THE HOLISTIC COOKBOOK

Eileen Renders N. D.
Renders Publishing

Renders Publishing

ISBN 0-9711551-0-0

The health information contained within this Holistic Cookbook is offered as a guide for current general information and is not intended to be used as a substitute for medical advice, diagnosis, or treatment.

Printed in the United States by Network Printers, Milwaukee, WI.

Publisher's Cataloging-in-Publication
(Provided by Quality Books, Inc.)

Renders, Eileen, 1939-
The holistic cook book / by Eileen Renders -- 1st ed.
p. cm.
Includes bibliographical references and index.
ISBN: 0-9711551-0-0
1. Natural foods. 2. Cookery (Natural foods) 3. Nutrition. I. Title.
TX369 R46 2001 641.3'02
QBI01-200882

Contents

Dedication

This book is dedicated to my husband
Lucas. To him I will be forever grateful for
His ability to provide an environment steeped
In tranquility, thus promoting an atmosphere
Conducive to stimulating creativity, hence
The Holistic Cookbook.
A Toast to the man who loves to eat,
And to the foods that truly nourish, satisfy
And heal, body, mind and spirit!

Introduction

Eileen Renders N. D. (Doctor of Naturopathy) is the Author of The Holistic Cookbook, and in 1995 founded RENDERS WELLNESS in Egg Harbor Township, New Jersey where she has continued to provide Consultations In her Specialties; Nutritional Therapy and Herbal Medicine.

She has provided Health articles for several newspapers And National magazines. Eileen Renders has provided Therapeutic Alternatives through Lectures, Writing and Classes. In 1998 her first book; "Food Additives, Nutrients And Supplements A To Z" was published by ClearLight Publishers. Her experience and expertise Has been acknowledged by such referrals as the renown CHILDREN'S HOSPITAL OF PA.'S Oncology Dept., The Atlantic City Medical Center's HIV Consortium, and Dozens of Doctors, Chiropractors and Nurses.

Eileen Renders N. D. might be most recognized For her expertise in working with individuals with a Compromised Immune system, such as individuals With cancer and HIV, or Hepatitis-C.

The Holistic Cookbook is published upon popular Demand from hundreds of individuals who are living with A serious disorder, or attempting to manage a chronic Disorder. Many of these individuals are now learning how To protect their Immune System through avoidance of Antagonists, including toxins ingested through pesticide Residues found on many of the commonly eaten foods, And other highly processed foods, all of which (when Consumed in excess) can contribute to Liver toxicity, And further compromising the Immune System. This is A Cookbook which will provide much valuable information For Colleges, Teachers, Students, Libraries, and all who Are interested in expanding both their knowledge and their Lives!

More recently, Renders Wellness has expanded their Interests and services through the addition of their new Publishing Department. Another confirmation of their Commitment to continue to create a nutritional awareness Through the development of an information vehicle to Insure same.

THE HOLISTIC COOK BOOK

by Eileen Renders N.D.

An overview of "How" many of us may not be eating as healthy as we would like to believe we are eating, and the association between denatured foods and disease.

While many Americans are just now beginning to understand the potential harm caused to the body as a result of excess consumption of Saturated fats, most have yet to take it upon themselves to address the difficult task of recognizing and eliminating other potential toxins which assault the body on a daily basis. The toxins of which I speak, often come to us in the form of highly processed foods and are contained in food additives and food preservatives of which the average Shopper knows little.

Knowing which food additives or food preservatives are safe and which can contribute to a toxic overload within the body can often mean the difference between a healthy Immune system or disease. This is especially true when one already suffers with a compromised Immune system, Liver disease, or Cancer.

And although many families truly have made the commitment to follow a healthier lifestyle which includes healthier eating, most are limited in achieving much success in terms of longevity due to a lack of available information on exactly "How" to do so. Unmasking those foods (and I use the word food lightly here) which can be associated with a higher health risk for various common disorders, such as CHD (Cardiovascular Heart Disease), Diabetes, Cancer and other diseases, simply does not assist us in overcoming the task of discerning which healthier food replacements are available to us, verses those traditional denatured favorites. And of course, we would like to be able to incorporate healthy substitutes, without compromising taste!

If this seems to be an enormous task for one to implement, consider this; Begin your transition by eliminating foods which are canned, boxed, or bagged. Replace them with fresh foods which have been cleaned, or by purchasing organic. This alone will immensely reduce the consumption of potent chemicals.

This is not only a transition for each of us for today, but will become an example of healthy eating which we will be passing Down from generation to generation.

Though individual tastes may vary, all the more one's sense of creativity can be motivated, once the tools are made available to each of us. The tools are not the cooking utensils in this cookbook, but the recipe replacement ingredients provided.

Scientific Studies often point to a number of foods that have been associated with increasing one's risk for developing CHD, Cancer and Diabetes, or the association between Colon cancer and a low fiber intake. But, seldom are we able to make the connection between specific mushrooms (such as Shiitake or Maitake) and Immune enhancement. Arteriosclerosis for instance, may indeed be a very preventable disease

While we understand how hydrogenated oils can clog the arteries, how many consumers are aware of the benefits associated with regular intake of the Essential Fatty Acids? By eliminating the chemicals and incorporating fresh foods into the diet which have been thoroughly rinsed (these products are now available at most Super Markets) and you will be protecting your Liver from what can be termed an "Accumulative effect" of toxins! A healthier Immune system is the result! High triglyceride levels (a type of fat in the blood) are directly affected by the amount of sugar consumed hour to hour. Candida also thrives in an acidic environment. yet how many homemakers think of sugar as an acid? Yet in fact it is! Hyperactive children often diagnosed ADHD usually snack on highly salted foods such as; Pretzels, chips, peanut-butter and etc. Sodium chloride (table salt) contains a good amount of Iodine, and excess ingestion of Iodine will directly affect the Thyroid gland, thus contributing to the hyper condition. Also, Sodium chloride (table salt) contains Aluminum which is used to prevent caking, and which of us would knowingly give our child Aluminum to ingest?

In this book, we have alphabetically lumped together various food types such as denatured foods. Also included in this directory are healthier replacements for mentioned denatured, and devitalized foods.

The recipes selected will in no way compromise one's enjoyment of the senses relative to smell, taste, or texture. With each recipe the reader will become more adept at understanding how to incorporate many of the healthier replacement foods mentioned in this book into many of their own favorite recipes! With the proper understanding, guidance and tools available to him/her, the reader will soon find themselves seeing food and health as synonymous, thus rekindling a renewed energy and imagination for creating recipes that will fulfill the purpose for which food has always been intended, that is; To nourish body, mind and soul.

The final pages of this book are devoted to providing access to many of the foods mentioned throughout this Holistic Cook Book, and in many of its recipes. Consider a few of the following healthy recipes; Tofu Cheesecake, Pumpkin muffins, Vanilla Soy shakes, Stuffed Lentil Peppers and many more!

Index To Chapters

INTRODUCTION

The Twentieth Century now has an ever-growing number of health conscious individuals and families who are ready and willing to make positive changes for the sake of maintaining good health. Now, more than ever before, we as consumers have many good reasons for concern regarding how as a Nation, we eat. During the First World War in the forties, many families experienced the loss of two parents; a father who temporarily belonged to Uncle Sam, and a mother, who for the first time in her life, went off to work. After a War, America usually enjoys an economical surge, and so it was in the forties! With growing technological abilities, the average family was motivated to keep up with the Jones', so Mom continued to remain a working mother. This created an atmosphere at home which often led to meals being served late, or a Mom who was often tired, and less available for her family. With her job career, her home and her family, there seemed little time left for household chores.

This often meant that dinner was less often prepared from scratch. And by the time the Fifties rolled around, many families now had a home Freezer that could hold up to a couple of weeks of prepared meals for the family. Super Markets joined in too, as did the Manufacturer's of processed foods. These processed foods could be taken right from the Freezer and popped directly into a preheated oven, and reach the Dining room table in less than forty-five minutes. It was a treat for Mom, and gave her a bit of an edge as far as time-management was concerned. About that same time, there seemed no more reason for standing at the kitchen stove all day, stirring a home made marinara sauce. Because that too, was now available for purchase at the local Super Market. Baking muffins, breads, or pies almost became a thing of the past with the availability of Commercially Baked goods. And the Food Additives, and Food Preservatives that were being used in these Bakery products helped to keep them fresh for days, sometimes as long as a week or more! Other foods gave the new working Mother a break too!

There were many boxed cereals, canned vegetables, and bagged Snack foods making their way to the Super Markets. They were a big hit with the kids in everyone's home. Boxed, bagged, or canned, they were easy to store in the Kitchen cabinets. No longer did vegetables require cleaning, peeling, chopping, or lengthy cooking procedures. Not at all, many were pre-cooked. Sodium content was always a bit high in these types of Prepared or Processed Foods, but Americans enjoyed the taste of salt. And who was reading labels anyway? After all, Ingredient labels had not yet made their way into the Marketplace until much later.

With Fifties, the U.S. dollar was stronger than ever. Indeed, technology had come a long way, and Computers were beginning to make their way into the Workplace. Many families owned a family car, and were able to travel with their family places where they could not have gone together as a family before. The Coal Furnace that was once used to heat the family home was long gone. No more tending to the fire, chopping wood, or working to maintain a consistent temperature throughout the home.

The Fifties brought to the majority of families, the convenience of owning a Central Heating Unit. Thermostatically controlled heat was a luxury! Let's see now; no more Victory Gardens, no more chopping wood, or burning coal in the Coal Furnace, what next?

Into the Sixties we were hurled, and the affluent now could enjoy Air conditioning when the temperatures soared. Remember those frozen pizzas? Well, the family could then take them from the freezer, heat them quickly in this new gadget making its way onto the scene, it was called a Microwave. Some worried a bit about the magnetic waves they created, or if they could cause any harm to us, but those fears were quickly allayed by the sheer convenience they provided the Family on the go!

But, the more technology advanced, the more our parents had to work, or be away from home *in order to keep up with the neighbors.* Divorce was at an all time high in the Fifties and Sixties, and that created a new need for women to find their independence, an equality in the Work Place, hence "The Women's Liberation Movement" was born. The working mothers of the Fifties encouraged their own daughters to get a good education (which up until that time had been only thought necessary to the male members of the Family, other than the affluent), to go to College, and to secure their own independence in the World.

While the "Latch Key" kids were never really noticed until the late Seventies or early Eighties, they were probably born out of the early Sixties.

In the Seventies,, a twelve year old was now capable of doing his, or her own Laundry, thanks to the Automatic Washing Machines and Dryers present in every home. No need to break buttons on the Wringer Washing Machine's rollers, nor to be present at all while this whole process known as the laundry was being done.

Americans enjoyed this new Life Style, it was easier than it had been for their parents, and made everyday household chores a thing of the past. There was no more sweeping, mopping, or waxing of floors; we now had wall-to-wall carpeting throughout, and an electric Vacuum Cleaner to take care of the picking up. And it was all accomplished with just the click of a little button! Life had certainly gotten easier for the modern American woman, and who could blame her for enjoying this life of luxury? What most of us did not realize way back then however, was how potentially harmful to our families many of these Processed foods might be! We experienced growth so quickly you see, that our big brothers the FDA (The Food and Drug Administration) were unable to keep up with the hundreds of new Food Additives, and Food Preservatives that were flooding the Market Place. They had their hands full trying to stay on top with the many new Drugs that were also being "Approved."

Their approach (the FDA) was to "Allow" these Food Additives at restricted levels where they felt they would not become harmful for human consumption.

A problem later developed however, when no one could have predicted just how many of these Additives would find their way into the foods that our Families would be consuming on a regular basis. In other words; The idea of going over the FDA'S allowable or permitted doses (regarding these Additives) through the consumption of many such foods on a daily basis, had not yet been considered. Nor had these "Experts" had any foresight regarding the possibility of their "Accumulative effect" upon those individuals who ate many types of specific foods containing these Additives and/or Preservatives on a regular basis.

So who is the FDA? The Food and Drug Administration is an Agency appointed by the Government to examine, review, and approve, or disapprove the Food Additives, Food Preservatives, including Drugs that find their way to the FDA for "Approval" each year.

Besides the potential harm associated with excess ingestion of foods containing specific Additives and Preservatives, we are often consuming to excess other substances which can contribute to the onset of Nutritional deficiencies at best, or even serious disease such as Cancer.

While our Country has continued to spend billions of dollars in the last few decades for Researching the cure for Cancer, and Heart disease, no cures have been found! In fact, Cancer and Heart diseases remain the two #1 causes of death. Some Health Experts in fact, are predicting that by the year 2010, over thirty or forty million more new cases of Diabetes will be diagnosed, yet often times, this is a disease of Adult onset which can be prevented through good Nutrition, exercise and maintaining one's ideal weight. Perhaps there is no better time than now for us, as a Nation, to reconsider the idea of retracing our steps backward. Back to a time when our vegetables were home grown, and not sprayed with herbicides and pesticides, many of which are known carcinogens.

Back to a time when people were more active, walking or riding a bicycle was common- place. Back to when people cooked a meal from "Scratch", rather than relying on processed foods, the Freezer, or the Microwave oven. Back to when a homemade cake did not list thirty ingredients on a label, yet only three of those ingredients were recognizable as real food!

Yet we would be going back also, to a time when many of the diseases of today were literally unheard of. That was when we had healthy Immune Systems, and did not compromise our Immune System by overloading the body with toxins.

In this Holistic Cook Book, we will take a closer look at the differences between processed foods, and fresh or whole foods. We will examine the many "Traditional" foods that line the food shelves in our Super Markets today, (those foods which when consumed to excess can interfere with optimum health) and attempt to provide healthier food replacements without sacrificing taste!

In other words, while we are aware of how refined white sugar, or refined white flours are not only void of essential nutrients, and how they might contribute to common disorders (or agitate many chronic disorders) such as Obesity, Heart Disease, Diabetes, Atherosclerosis and etc., many individuals have yet to find healthier replacements for these devitalized foods.

This book will not only provide healthier substitutes for these traditional denatured foods, but will provide a nutritional profile of these foods.

Several Research Universities are studying the healing benefits of many foods, including those associated with Soy, Oolong tea (Chinese green tea), Tumeric and others. We will not only provide the reader with some of that information, but we will offer a few tasty recipes along with that information, such as *Cheesecake made with silken tofu and Low-Fat Ricotta cheese!*

If we are what we eat, and an ounce of prevention is worth a pound of cure, then here is a Cook Book which will help to provide the vehicle of transport for the transitional process from "denatured, or devitalized" back toward the health, and Immune enhancement benefits often referred to as "Holistic", or "Natural Healing abilities."

In Chapter Two of this book, we will include a glossary of *ingredients,* which can be utilized by the reader who is interested in the nutritional profile of these commonly used foods and/or ingredients. Along with each recipe, at the bottom of each page, there may be a recipe contributor's name, or author's comment regarding healing powers of the recipe's ingredients.

This Cook Book will include a chapter on whole grains, flours, and beans. It will briefly discuss the various types of Organic, or Unbleached Whole grain flours, their main components, and how they can lend themselves to various dishes. For instance; Millet flour is obtained from a whole grain, and contains more Potassium in a comparable portion, than a banana, and it can be cooked in the same way as rice to make a pudding!

We will also cover which nutrients might be lacking in many geographical areas, due to soil depletion of such nutrients. And we will make suggestions for how to obtain a daily requirement of such essentials, such as *Trace Minerals.* While the foods and recipes in this Cook Book do not guarantee complete protection against such diseases as Cancer, many studies do show however, that the risk may be cut dramatically by as much as fifty percent! It will discuss the best and worse of Oils, as well as those which are considered to be more often associated with Heart Disease , or Atherosclerosis and Arteriosclerosis, including the association between *Hydrogenated oils and Cancer.*

The new Holistic cook will find tips on how to make the gradual transition from present day to optimum wellness, without creating havoc in the home. Just as the reader will become more aware of which foods are known to possess healing properties, so too, will the reader begin to recognize which types of foods to limit, or eliminate altogether! Alternatives will always be available, and the reader will be provided with more than one choice whenever available.

It is the Author's hope to provide pure nourishing whole foods of the type which can compliment many health goals, and life styles, including the type of nutritional fortification for those individuals who may be undergoing Chemotherapy for Cancer.

CHAPTER ONE

FOOD ADDITIVES

"Why" We May Not Be Eating As Healthy As We Believe We Are Eating.

In this chapter we will be taking a closer look at many of the foods that fall into the category of denatured, or devitalized, and contain food additives, preservatives, hydrogenated oils, food colorings, or synthetic hormones, including chemicals which could be detrimental to our health. Yet these are the very foods that are often those which are commonly eaten in the average household on a regular basis. Whoever said; "Ignorance is bliss" was not telling the truth, and time has proven that "The truth will set you free!" Inasmuch as the opportunity presents itself , our ability to make sound choices regarding food and nutrition is relative to available evidence of which, it is the Author's hope to present you with in The Holistic Cookbook.

The subject content is a subject near and dear to the hearts of everyone, and is the subject for which decisions are made on a daily basis by all of us! Often those decisions are unconscious, and we are oblivious to the obvious fact that food (and I use that word loosely here) has the potential to either literally make, or break us!

Yet we read, or hear so much jargon from the News Media today, we are often unable to properly decipher what is true, and what is not! In this chapter, Food Additives and Food Preservatives are the topic. Understanding what one must avoid, or eliminate from the diet certainly involves knowledge. In order to nourish the body properly, healthy decisions are required regarding the types of food we put into our body. The empowerment intended for the public, and in particular the readers of The Holistic Cookbook is to educate the Shopper regarding which types of Additives are potential toxins, as well as others which are relatively safe. When this information has been absorbed, the next chapter will actually provide the next big step towards reaching maximum health and preventing disease, it will not only list the most commonly eaten denatured foods, but it will also offer suggestions for healthier replacements. *Quite often, the Food Additives or Food Preservatives listed in this chapter are associated with many common health disorders when consumed in excess, and can often contribute to a weakening of the body's Immune System.*

Because there are hundreds upon hundreds of chemical substances that are utilized as Food Additives, or Food Preservatives which have many uses, we will provide you with an overview of their Classifications, and uses.

Bleaching Agents~ For five decades Processors have been adding bleaching agents to white flour in order to speed up the maturing process, thereby cutting their storage costs. When flour is freshly ground it is a pale yellow in color. As it ages, it begins to turn whiter in color, and its baking qualities are improved. Chemical substances such as chlorine dioxide, oxides of nitrogen, and nitrosyl chloride have the ability of both whitening, and maturing compounds that save Manufacturers thousands of dollars annually. These oxide compounds are said to be "Improving" agents. Other foods in which these bleaching agents are used include some types of cheese.

Coloring Agents~ These are additives that are used in order to enhance the appeal of particular foods. They are used in two forms; Synthetic and natural. Many Experts contend that these additives may conceal the actual quality of a particular product, and therefore mislead consumers. The World Health Organization (WHO), which is an Agency that has been delegated by the FDA (Food And Drug Administration) to review these food additives, and report back to them with their findings, believes that a great many of these food coloring agents may be hazardous to our health. Presently, there are approximately 140 different types of food coloring agents being used in various food products across the United States. In 1960 it was required by the Federal Government that these various food-coloring agents be retested in order to be approved as "Harmless." This law became mandatory due to the fact that many of the food-coloring agents already in use were found to be toxic when fed to animals. At this writing, only about nine, or ten have been "Proven to be safe."

However, FD and C Blue No. 1 and FD and Citrus Red No. 2 have caused tumors in animals after being injected under the skin. FD and Red No. 40 are significantly used food colorings that are now being examined further by Scientists who believe it should never have been given the GRAS (Generally Regarded As Safe) status because all of the information which regarded these coloring agents as "Safe" were carried out by the Manufacturer. The FDA'S contention is this; Since the studies that showed these coloring agents to be harmful when injected under the skin, their findings are irrelevant to how they are presently being used as coloring agents in foods.

Emulsifiers~ Employed to stabilize, and maintain consistency, it prevents separating. Two of the most widely used emulsifiers are Polysorbate 60, and lecithin. Lecithin made from pure Soy granules is not only safe, but is very nutritional, while the other, Polysorbate 60 is associated with 1, and 4 dioxane, a substance known to cause cancer in animals.

Flavorings~ Because processing of foods is known to deplete foods of their individual taste, more than two-thirds flavorings. It is said that of these two thousand flavorings, only about five hundred are "Natural", the balance being synthetic. Their consistency ranges from a sparsely few parts per million to as much as several hundred parts per million. There are also what is known as Flavor enhancer's, and some have names such as; Carvone, ethyl butyrate, or Benzaldehyde. MSG, or monosodium glutamate is one that is familiar to most because of the many allergic responses it produced to individuals who were hypersensitive to this substance.

Preservatives~ Whenever a preservative is incorporated into a fatty food type, it is referred to as an "Antioxidant." Antioxidants are those preservatives (such as BHA, or butylated hydroxyanisole) which are useful in retarding the development of offending odors, or tastes. BHA is most commonly found in such foods as; Crackers, potato chips, or prepared soups. Another type of preservative is one that is used to inhibit microbiological spoilage and chemical degradation. Other preservatives such as those found in breads, or bakery products are employed (such as calcium propionate) for preventing mold. Preservatives are also used to inhibit fungus growth on citrus fruits, they are known as fungicides.

Still another type of preservative are the "Sequestering Agents", and they are used in foods for protecting the food from chemical changes relative to its texture, color, or appeal. These found in soft drinks, and dairy products. Some of these sequestering agents are; Sodium calcium, and potassium salts of citric, pyrophosphoric, and tartaric acids.

Processing Chemical Agents~ Under this broad heading falls many types of chemical categories such as; Clarifying agents, Emulsifiers, and Emulsion Stabilizers, Thickeners, and Texturizers. Tannin for instance, is used for clarifying liquids in both the brewing, and in the wine industry. Emulsifiers assist in maintaining consistency of a food composition, such as in Bakery products, or frozen desserts.

Reducing Agent~ These are substances which have the ability to reduce a volume mixture, thereby creating a concentrated preparation. Their main use as an Additive in food is to prevent metals from oxidizing, thus negatively affecting their taste, or color, such as in fats, and oils.

Solvent~ This additive is a liquid solution which has the ability to dissolve several substances, making it a joined mixture of equal texture, or consistency.

Texturizer~ A compound employed to enhance the texture of a food, such as canned vegetables. Calcium chloride is a texturizer when added to a prepared food, helps to maintain its firmness.

Note: In the glossary section (located at the end of Chapter one), more information is provided on the FDA, the WHO, and other Regulatory Agencies whose responsibility it is, to manage control over those chemical substances referred to as "Food Additives, and Food Preservatives."

Acetate~ This substance is considered irritating to the stomach when consumed in large quantities. It is also known as the salt of acetic acid, and is often found in dessert and bakery products, including such beverages as coffee, and liquors. It is also commonly found in cookies, pastries, and candy.

Alginic Acid~ Used as a stabilizer, alginic acid is a gelatinous precipitate derived from seaweed. It is commonly found in such foods as; Ice cream, frozen ices, cheeses, cheese spreads, and salad dressings. Gradually soluble in water, it forms a thick liquid. The World Health Organization (WHO) found that when fifteen percent alginate was added to the diet of rats for three months, fifteen percent of the rats developed an enlarged lower intestine, a bumpy urinary bladder, and deposits of calcium within the pelvic wall. The FDA'S PAFA (Priority Based Assessment of Food Additives) has not completed a search on available literature regarding the toxicology of this additive.

Allyl Sulfide~ A flavoring agent of synthetic composition, Allyl Sulfide is found in many beverages, including ice cream, candy, and bakery products. This synthetic agent is also found in many condiments, and some types of meat. It can cause irritation to the eyes, and respiratory tract, and is easily absorbable through the skin. Excessive, or continued exposure can cause kidney and liver damage.

Aluminum Potassium Sulfate~ These translucent crystals and powders are used for clarifying sugar. This chemical compound is also employed in the making of bleached flours, pickles, cereals, and cheeses. Large amounts can cause burning in the mouth, and throat, along with irritation of the stomach. But, the last report in 1980 from the Select Committee to the FDA on GRAS (Generally Regarded As Safe) product status of this substance was that it should continue to be used without any limitations whatsoever, other than good manufacturing practices.

Benomyl~ (Methyl-l-{butyl carbamoyl}-2-benzimidazole-carbamate).Tersan 1991. Bonide. A generic name for a fungicide that is used on various fruits after they have been picked, such as peaches and apples. Tolerance levels for this chemical have been set by the FDA at the following Parts per million; 70 ppm for dried apple pomace resulting from application to apples, 50 ppm on raisins resulting from application to growing grapes, 50 ppm in concentrated tomato products resulting from application to growing crop, and 125 ppm in dried grape pomace and raisin waste resulting from application to growing grapes. It is believed to cause birth defects, and is somewhat of an irritant to the skin. This chemical is highly toxic when ingested.

Benzin~ Derived from coal tar and oil, this additive has several uses which include the following; as a solvent, and for managing color. Often used as a protective coating on fruits and eggshells, it is known to cause dizziness, loss of appetite, and headaches with long time exposure. If injected into the vein of a human being, benzin could prove to be fatal! Yet the FDA permits its use without any limitation other than "It should not be used in excess of an amount reasonably required for accomplishing intended use."

Bifenthrin~ A pesticide of synthetic pyrethroid nature, it is used to control insects and mites. Tolerance levels as set by the FDA are as follows; 0.10 ppm (parts per million) in meat, fat, and meat byproducts of goats, sheep and cattle, 0.02 ppm in milk.

Borneol~ Employed as a flavoring agent, it has a distinct peppery odor, and a burning taste. It is found naturally in coriander, rosemary, strawberries, nutmeg, and oil of lime. It is used however, synthetically as a spice flavoring in ice cream, candies, chewing gum and bakery products. It has a toxicity level which parallels that of camphor oil, and can initiate nausea, vomiting, confusion, dizziness and convulsions.

Bromo Methane~ Employed as a fumigant in feed used for animals, and in barley, cereal grains, corn, rice, fava beans, flour, kiwi fruit, lentils, oats, nuts, wheat, rye, and sweet potatoes. Residue tolerances set by the FDA are as follows; 125 ppm (parts per million) for cereal grains, including barley, corn, grain sorghum, oats, wheat, rice and rye when used for animal feed. It is "Allowed" at 25 ppm in fermented malt beverages. This fumigant is highly toxic, especially by inhalation. Lung irritation follows acute poisoning, leading to death. Death caused by injury to the Central Nervous System is caused by chronic poisoning.

Butyl Acetate~ A synthetic flavoring agent also known by the names Acetic acid and Butyl Ester. Utilized as a flavoring for butter, beverages, candy, ice cream and bakery products, It can also be found in various gelatin desserts. It is also a component employed in the manufacture of lacquer, plastic, and safety glass. In large amounts, this compound becomes a narcotic, and is toxic when inhaled in amounts equaling 200 ppm (parts per million.)

Butyl Alcohol~ A synthetic flavoring agent used in making ice cream, baked goods, candy, various beverages, cordials, liquor, and cream. It occurs naturally in raspberries and apples. Again, it is employed as a clarifying agent in shellac, fats, waxes, and shampoos. It is known to lead to irritation of the mucous membranes, including headache and dizziness. As little as 25 ppm (parts per million) can lead to pulmonary disorders in humans.

Calcium Chloride~ This substance is used for its texturizing abilities, and as a drying agent. It can be found in canned tomatoes, in apple pie mix, in artificially sweetened jellies, and also as a firming agent for various cheeses. Medicinally, it has been used for its diuretic abilities, and as a urinary acidifier, or balancer. But, it can also be found in the ingredients used for preserving wood, or for melting ice. Known to cause hear and stomach disorders upon ingestion. The Select Committee on GRAS Substances reported in 1980 that Calcium chloride should continue its GRAS Status with no limitations, other than good manufacturing practices.

Calcium Iodate~ Employed as a dough conditioner for making rolls, buns, and breads, it can be a nutritional source of iodine. Though it is not highly toxic us , it has caused allergic responses. A Toxicology study has done yet been completed by the FDA.

Calcium Lactate~ A substance incorporated into many types of Baking powder, and as a dough conditioner, it has also been employed medicinally for the treatment of Calcium deficiencies. However, it very well might lead to cardiac, or gastrointestinal disorders. In 1980 the Select Committee reported to the FDA that this chemical substance should continue its GRAS (Generally Regarded As Safe) status, and set no limitations for its manufacturing practices, other than the usual "Good Manufacturing Practices."

Cepharpirin~ A drug used for animals, it is allowed at specific tolerance levels as set by the FDA in both beef, and milk. The FDA limits set for uncooked edible tissues of cattle at 0.1 ppm (parts per million), and 0.02 ppm residues for milk. Injection via the vein produces a moderate toxicity, and if heated to decomposition, it releases toxic fumes.

Cholecarciferol~ Used as a dietary supplement and nutrient in cereals, and is a synthetic source for Vitamin D-3. It can also be found in pasta, milk, margarine, and some grain products. It is poison by ingestion, and may cause birth defects.

Coal Tar~ Derived from bituminous coal, this thick semisolid liquid known as coal tar, has many chemical constituents within its composition, including; benzene, cresol, naphthalene, phenol, quinolineoline, and xylenes. Coal tar is found in some food preservatives, woodworking, synthetic flavorings, adhesives, and insecticides. Coal tar is known to cause cancer in animals, and very often is the cause of allergic responses in those who are sensitive.

Coumaphos~ This chemical substance might be found listed under such names as **Bamboos 50, Asunthol, or Agridip.** An insecticide used to kill worms, it is added to the feed of animals. However, it is highly poisonous either by ingestion, or injection, or through inhalation. It is thought to be a mutagen.

Dihydrocoumarin~ A synthetic flavoring used in the manufacture of many fruits and liquors, it is also used in ice cream, baked goods, candy, and other desserts. The FDA'S Data Bank PAFA has more information available upon request regarding the toxicology of this substance. However, continued use of this chemical might be a potential cause of Liver damage.

Dodecylbenzenesulfonic Acid~ Employed for sanitizing glass milk containers, this chemical is known as a detergent. If ingested, it can produce vomiting, and can cause a rash when in contact with the skin. The FDA allows a residue of less than 400 ppm (parts per million) in solution.

Endosulfan~ Thiodan. Derived from methane and benzene, this chemical is related to DDT which has been banned, but is still very much present in the environment. It is utilized as a pesticide on many fruits and vegetables, including tomatoes, carrots, lettuce, and many others. The FDA limits a residue of 24 ppm for dried tea.

This lethal chemical is toxic whether inhaled, ingested, or through skin absorption. Studies however, show that this chemical, along with others which attempt to mimic the human reproductive hormone known as estrogen may be associated with breast cancer, although sufficient proof may be lacking.

FD And C Blue No.1, FD And C Blue No. 1 Aluminum Lake, FD And C Blue No. 2, FD And C Citrus Red No. 2, FD And C Green No. 1, FD And C Green No.2, FD And C Green No. 3, FD And C Lakes, FD And C Red No. 2, FD And C Red No. 3, FD And C Red No. 3 Aluminum Lake, FD And C Red No. 4, FD And C Red No. 20, FD And C Red No. 22, FD And C Red No. 40, FD And C Violet No. 1, FD And C Yellow No. 5, FD And C Yellow No. 5 Aluminum Lake, FD And C Yellow No. 6, FD And C Yellow No. 6 Aluminum Lake.

FD And C Colors~ Food Colorings go back as far as the early 1900's when there were more than eighty different Food Colorings, and no regulations for their use were in place. These Colors are described as any dye, or additive which can change the Color of a Food, Drug, or Cosmetic product. In 1906, legislation put together its initial regulations for use of these dyes. In 1938 new legislation was passed, and that is when Colors were given Numbers, rather than their chemical names. Throughout the years, and up to this writing, much confusion regarding the safety of these Colorings has been debated, the result being that many have been banned. Though some of these Colorings have been shown to cause tumors in Laboratory animals, the FDA contends that the "Risk of Cancer" is

minimal, therefore, many are still in use. But, many groups, such as Ralph Nader's Public Citizen maintains that "Any risk at all, is unacceptable." At best, these
Food Colorings are often a source of Allergy producing symptoms in many hypersensitive individuals, and especially in children.

Fenvalerate~ Also found under the name of Sumifly, this insecticide is added to tomatoes and sunflower seeds that is fed to animals. Residue limitations are set at 0.05 ppm on all food products, and 20 ppm (parts per million) for animal feed. This chemical, and all of the chemicals which make up the compound known as Cyanide are made available to consumers on "The Right To Know List." Mildly toxic through contact to the skin, it is poison if ingested. It is extremely poisonous to bees and fish. And it is a corrosive which causes eye damage.

Note: While most Food Ingredients are listed on the exterior Ingredient label, and allow consumers the right to choose, or not to choose, based on information provided, these Insecticides are a good example of what we often consume, without knowledge, or consent!

Glyceryl Monostearate~ Incorporated into such foods as margarines, shortening and cosmetics, this compound is known as an Emulsifying and Dispersing agent. It can cause death to mice through large dose injections. The FDA is presently looking into the toxicology of this additive.

Guanylic Acid Sodium Salt~ Found in poultry, soups, and many canned foods, this compound is employed as a *flavor enhancer.* It is also known by the name Disodium Guanylate. If ingested, it is moderately toxic. In Laboratory animals, it has caused mutations.

Heptanal~ A derivative of Castor oil, Heptanal, or Heptaldehyde is a synthetic, or artificial flavoring agent. Often found in rum, cognac, and liqueurs, it is also often present in ice cream, candies, and bakery products, among other foods. It moderately toxic through ingestion, and the FDA/s Data Bank (PAFA) has more information available regarding the toxicology of this additive upon request.

Hydrogen Cyanide~ Used as a fumigant in cereal flours, cocoa, and in meats such as bacon, or ham. It is also used by Veterinarians in a preparation for treating inflammation of udders. The FDA permits residue tolerances for this substance at varying levels, and allows residues for as much as 200 ppm (parts per million) in cocoa, 90 ppm in cereals cooked before eaten, and 50 ppm in uncooked ham, bacon, or sausage. Large, or continued exposure in humans can cause shortness of breath, unconsciousness, convulsions, and pulmonary arrest. An exposure of 150 ppm for as little as half an hour could seriously injure human beings, and an exposure of 300 ppm for only a few minutes could result in death! Exterminating of rats is accomplished by using a compressed gas from this chemical. It is so lethal, only a trained expert can safely handle this compressed gas.

Hydrogenated Oil~ A process whereby a naturally occurring polyunsaturated is heated to extreme temperatures that results in turning these polyunsaturated fats into semisolid saturated fats.

Hydrogenated oils have been shown to adversely affect the fat levels in the blood, and have been associated with colon cancer, according to some studies.

Isoamyl Acetate~ Utilized as a flavoring, this compound is very often found in such foods as; Baked goods, beverages, fruit flavorings, candy, ice cream, cola, and many other similar type foods. In chewing gum, the FDA allows as much as 2,700 ppm (parts per million). However, as much as 950 ppm for sixty minutes has resulted in fatigue, headache, and irritation of the mucous membranes. The FDA has more toxicology information regarding this additive for Consumers, upon request.

Isoeugenol~ A synthetic flavoring agent, this substance is used in the making of everything from bakery goods to spices and condiments. It is also used in the manufacture of vanillin, and is mildly toxic by ingestion. It is allowed in chewing gum at residue levels of 1,000 ppm, yet has been responsible for causing mutations in Laboratory animals.

Magnesium Oxide~ This additive has been employed for various uses, including the following; A firming agent, lubricant, releasing agent, anti-caking agent, and a neutralizing agent. It is found in dairy products, and canned peas, and in several other food products. It is thought to be responsible for causing tumors in human beings, and is being researched regarding its safety by the FDA. Breathing in of this chemical caused fever.

Maleic Acid~ Often employed as a preservative used in oils, it is toxic by ingestion. More information is available on Maleic Acid upon request from the FDA'S Data Bank.

Menadione~ This substance in prohibited as a dietary supplement for humans, but is used as a vitamin K-3 supplement (in their feed) for turkeys, chicken, and pigs. This synthetic substance is shown to have vitamin K properties, and is used for preventing a vitamin K deficiency in the above named animals, and is also used in milk products to prevent souring. It can be irritating to respiratory passages, mucous membranes, and the skin.

Methyl Chloride~ Also goes by the name of Chloromethane. With somewhat of a sweet taste, this compound is used as a pesticide spray in processing areas, and in food storage areas. This chemical is toxic, and can serious damage to the kidneys, and liver, or result in death.

Methylbenzene Acetate~ Employed as a flavoring in many foods, this substance has a sweet smell which resembles that of jasmine. Through ingestion, or by skin, this substance is mildly toxic.

Nitrate and Nitrites~ These two similar chemical substances are either *Sodium, or Potassium Nitrates, and/or Nitrites* which are used in Smoked meats, and foods such as; Vienna sausages, tuna fish, meat spreads, bacon, hot dogs, and bologna as a "Color fixative." They impart a fresh looking red-blooded appearance which helps to add a special palatable appeal to their eye-appeal. Much research has been done regarding the safety of these compounds, and the results indicate that when Nitrates, and Nitrites combine with the body's digestive saliva in the stomach, secondary "amines" are created, *and they are known to be powerful cancer-causing agents called nitrosamines.* The U.S. Department of Agriculture has power over Processed meats, and The FDA (Food Drug and Food Administration) resides over the manufacturing procedures with regard to poultry, and other types of food containing these chemicals.

The amount of data relative to these chemicals is quite lengthy, but can be obtained by interested Consumers who request it from the FDA'S Data Bank.

Note: *When eating foods containing these cancer-causing agents, include a sufficient dose of vitamin-C, which is thought to block the forming of some of the nitrosamines.*

Olestra~ Also known as Sucrose Polyester. Olestra was created as a Fat substitute, and is said to eliminate many of the calories, and previous problems associated with high fat intake in the diet. Olestra is not digested by the body, and is now being used in such products as; Potato chips, French fries, and other baked goods. There have been claims that it can cause diarrhea, and is reportedly said to promote liver changes, and tumors in animals.

Peroxide~ Benzoyl, Calcium, and Hydrogen. These various forms of peroxide are used in several different ways, and for just as many different results. *Benzoyl peroxide* for instance, is utilized in oils, cheese, and flours as a bleaching agent. *Calcium peroxide* is employed as a conditioner, and oxidizing agent for making rolls, breads, and buns. *Hydrogen peroxide, or dioxide* is incorporated into food starch as a modifier, and as a preservative, and bacterial inhibitor in milk and cheese. It is a compound that can harm the skin and eyes of humans, and is on the FDA list of additives to be studied for mutagenic, sub acute, and reproductive effects.

Phenol~ Many Manufacturers use phenol as an ingredient in food additives, or processing aids. It is a general disinfectant, and antiseptic. Small amounts of phenol, if swallowed, can induce vomiting, paralysis, convulsions, coma, respiratory failure, and cardiac arrest. The FDA (Food and Drug Administration) has more up-to-date information regarding the toxicology of this additive.

Polyoxyethylene Stearate~ A combination of Stearic acid and ethylene oxide. " texturizer" that was banned in 1952 when it was used in bread to make it feel softer, or fresher. In Laboratory animals, it caused tumors, and bladder stones.

Potassium Bromate~ Employed as an additive in breads to impart a spongy quality, along with the action of oxygen. "Allowed" as a flour treatment at 50 ppm (parts per million) until 1993, as the WHO (World Health Organization) Committee on Food Additives pointed to recent data which proved that Potassium Bromate caused kidney tumors, thyroid tumors, and other stomach cancers in Laboratory animals. With this new information demonstrating that this chemical, which had long been an additive was a mutagen, it was no longer allowed as an additive in the making of flour.

Profenofos~ Most commonly used in animal feed as a pesticide, it is *allowed* at up to 6 ppm for cottonseed hulls.

Propyl Propionate~ A synthetic flavoring additive used in banana, peach, apple, prune, and plum, and is often found in ice cream, candy, and some beverages, including rum. While the FDA has set limitations for this Additive is used in foods and spices, many of these allowances appear to be quite liberal. For instance; The FDA set limits at five percent for alcoholic beverages, two and a half percent (not ppm, or parts per million) in frozen dairy products, ninety seven percent in seasonings and flavorings, and five percent for nuts. This additive has caused birth defects in experiments with Laboratory animals, and the EPA (Environmental Protection Agency) has this substance listed in its Genetic Toxicology Program. The FDA can provide more relative information regarding this substance from it data bank.

Salicylic Acid~ Synthetically concocted through the combining of heated phenol and carbon dioxide. Salicylic Acid however, does occur in nature, and is found in such plants as wintergreen, and a few others. Employed as both a preservative in food products, residues in milk are not permitted. This is another synthetic substance which is on the EPA'S Genetic Toxicology Program list. Absorbable via the skin, high volume absorption can cause abdominal pain, acidosis, mental disturbances, and skin rashes. Poison by ingestion, it has caused birth defects in experiments with animals

Sodium Chloride~ Also known as table salt. A pickling agent, meat preservative, and seasoning, it has also been used as an antiseptic in mouthwashes, soap, and eye lotions. While diluted solutions are not considered to be an irritant, upon drying, the skin area affected soon becomes dehydrated, and can become a source of irritation. While it is not considered toxic, it can have a negative effect upon individuals prone to hypertension. Some Experts believe that children who consume Snack foods with high sodium content on a regular basis might be over-stimulating the Thyroid glands due to the iodine content as contained in Sodium chloride. This being true, it could contribute to a condition known as hyper kinetic, which describes the hyperactive child. In 1980, the FDA'S Select Committee stated that sodium chloride should continue to remain on the GRAS (Generally Regarded As Safe) list, without any limitations, other than the usual "Good Manufacturing" practices. However, PAFA (The FDA'S Elected Data Bank resource for the toxicology of specific substances) is currently investigating information regarding the safety, and use of sodium chloride.

Sodium Propionate~ A food preservative often found in bakery products, and confections for inhibiting mold and fungus, Sodium propionate has been also used medicinally for skin funguses, but has caused allergic responses. The FDA'S Data Bank (PAFA) knows of no reported use of this chemical, and has no toxicology information available regarding Sodium propionate.

Sorbitan Monostearate~ This food additive has a variety of uses; A defoamer, a flavoring, and dispersing agent, and an emulsifier. It is often found as an additive in the following types of foods: Cake mixes, milk substitutes, coffee, beverages, bakery products, cake fillings, and icing. Allowable ppm (parts per million) range from one percent to 0.0006 percent. There are no reported cases of injury from this additive. Human beings have ingested twenty grams in a single dose, without harm. The FDA has more comprehensive information available regarding this additive through their data bank

(PAFA).

Soybean Oil ~ Flour~ The oil is extracted from the seeds of a plant which grows in Asia, and the Midwestern part of the United States. And the oil is comprised of nearly 40 percent protein.

It is used as a "defoamer" in the manufacture of beet sugar. But is also employed in the manufacture of products such as: Margarine, candy, soap, and some shortenings. Today it lends itself in the manufacture of soy sauce, substitutes for milk and cheese (for vegetarians), and now is available in yogurt and other foods as a protein source. Though it may cause an allergic response to those who may be super-sensitive to soy, it is considered to be safe, and according to the Select Committee's Report to the FDA in 1980, they stated that Soybean oil should continue to enjoy its GRAS status with no limitations, other than the expected "Good manufacturing" standards.

Note: Soybean oil is sometimes heated at extreme temperatures whereby its unsaturated fat is turned into saturated fats through a process known as hydrogenation. The same processing is often carried out with cottonseed oil, and when an ingredient label reads hydrogenated, partially-hydrogenated, Soybean or Cottonseed oil, or any other type of hydrogenated oils, they become harmful!

Stanilo~ Spectinomycin. Employed as an antibiotic in chickens, residues of 0.1 are the permitted amount allowed, as per the FDA. Stanilo is also used medicinally in humans for the treatment of syphilis, however in large doses this substance can induce fever, chills, and decreased urine output.

Stannous Chloride~ Also known as Tin Dichloride. Utilized in the manufacture of canned foods such as sodas, or vegetables, it is an extremely effective reducing agent In 1980 the FDA'S Data Bank (PAFA) approved this chemical's continued GRAS (Generally Regarded As Safe). Stannous chloride has a low systemic toxic level, but is very irritating to mucous membranes, and the skin. This substance is on the FDA list of substances for more in-depth studies to determine its potential as a mutagenic, and/or its effects upon the reproductive organs.

Stearic Acid, or Octadecanoic Acid ~ Prepared synthetically through a process known as hydrogenation utilizing cottonseed, or other similar types of vegetable oils, it is also found in nature in some vegetable oils, and from an extract derived from cascarilla bark. As an "Additive" it is a texturizer which imparts a softness to baked goods, candy, and beverages, including chewing gum. It is often an ingredient found in foundation creams, antiperspirants, hair straighteners, shaving creams, and suppositories. The Select Committee reported to the FDA in 1980 that this substance should continue with its GRAS (Generally Regarded As Safe) status without limitations, other than the usual recommended "Good Manufacturing Practices." An irritant to human skin upon contact, it is a potential allergen to individuals with sensitivities. Researchers at the University of Texas reported in 1988 to the New England Journal of Medicine that this substance did not raise blood cholesterol levels as much as saturated fats, however that statement in itself is not very appealing, if that is the "Best" that can be said about these acids. The FDA'S Data Bank will have more information regarding the toxicology of this Additive available upon request.

Succinic Acid~ Utilized as a neutralizing agent in processed foods, it is also a buffer. It is manufactured from acetic acid, and employed as an ingredient in perfumes, mouthwash, and lacquers. In nature, it is present in fungi, and fossils. While there appears to be no known toxicity when used in cosmetics, large doses have been fatal to frogs when injected beneath the skin. Medicinally, it is used in the making of some types of laxatives. In 1980, The Select Committee reported to the FDA that Succinic acid should continue to be used without limitations on the GRAS (Generally Regarded As Safe) list. However, the PAFA (The FDA'S Data Bank) has not yet done a full study on the toxicology literature regarding this substance, and its relationship as a Food Additive.

Tallow Flakes ~ Also known as Suet. Firmer than grease, it is extracted from fatty tissue of bovine cattle and sheep in North America. As a "Food Additive", it is used as a defoaming agent in the manufacture of beet sugar. Employed also, as an ingredient in the manufacture of cosmetics, shaving creams, and soaps. However, adding tallow to the feed of miniature pigs for one year, caused Atherosclerosis (impaired blood flow due to clogging) in varying degrees of moderate to severe. It was noted that the developing Atherosclerosis was much like the type that develops in humans. However, in 1980, The Select Committee reported to the FDA that Tallow flakes should continue its GRAS (Generally

Regarded As Safe) status, without any limitations, other than those recommended for Standard Good Manufacturing Practices.

Tannic Acid~ Used medicinally for its astringent abilities, it occurs in nature, and can be found in the fruit and bark of many plants, especially in the bark of the oak, or sumac. It also is present in coffee, teas, and in cherries. The FDA permits tannic acid to be used in bakery products, liquor, butter, flavorings, beverages, and etc. at 1,000 ppm (parts per million). While it has a low toxicity level when ingested, excessive intake can often inhibit the body's ability to store iron. Tannic acid is antagonistic to iron. In Laboratory studies, large dose injections can cause tumors. Being reviewed by EPA (Environmental Protection Agency) Toxicology Program, and the International Agency for Research on Cancer (IARC). In 1980, the Select Committee reported to the FDA that Tannic acid should continue its GRAS (Generally Regarded As Safe) status, and that it considered safe when used as it is now.

Tergitol~ Also known by the names of Sodium Etasulfate and Tergemist. The FDA permits use of this substance as a cleaning agent with residues not to exceed 0.2 percent in solution with water. Utilized for cleaning of fruits, vegetables, and poultry, it is toxic by ingestion, and is known to cause injury to the skin, or eyes when contact is made.

Tetrachlorvinphos~ While the FDA permits the use of this chemical substance, it sets limits for residues at 0.00015 pound for each 100 pounds per body weight of horses, and cattle when used in animal feed. It is utilized as an insecticide in animal feed. In pigs its limitations are set at 0.00011 per hundred pounds of body weight per pig. This chemical substance is a white powdery compound that is able to inhibit the transmission of nerve signals, and was found to be a carcinogenic in animal feed by the National Cancer Institute. And it is also on the "Community Right To Know List." Highly toxic by ingestion. Its use on experimental animals resulted in reproductive disorders.

Xylenol~ A product derived from Coal tar, this substance also is known by the name 2-4- Dimethylphenol. Its uses are varied, and include the following; As a "Wetting-agent" in the manufacture of dyestuffs, a disinfectant in pharmaceuticals, and a solvent in insecticides, and a solvent used in the manufacture of rubber products. In Laboratory experiments with animals, it caused cancer when applied to the skin. The FDA Data Bank (PAFA) has more up to date information regarding the toxicology of this substance.

Zeranol, or Zearalanol~ Utilized in animals to aid in their growth, it is a hormone. The FDA sets a zero tolerance level for residue traces in the raw tissue of sheep and cattle.

Note: While the preceding list of food-additives and food-preservatives, including chemical substances such as insecticides, or hormones are offered as a way of promoting an awareness regarding the foods we eat, they are in no way meant to be construed as a complete listing.

CHAPTER TWO

Devitalized Food Favorites, And Healthier Replacements For Same

Beverages~ Under this heading we find those drinks which first come to mind, and are often the most consumed beverages in the average household. Coffee, Soft drinks, Teas, Milk and Juices.

Coffee~ A drink which contains caffeine, it supplies the body with zero nutrients. Caffeine is presently being studied further in order to determine whether, or not there is an association between Caffeine, and some types of Cancer. The Tannic Acid contained in Coffee, and black tea can also interfere with the body's ability to store, or make available certain nutrients, such as Iron. Expert Organizations such as (FAO) The Food and Agriculture Organization of the United Nations in order to share findings, and set standards, amongst other agenda items, and these two Committee's are in agreement with the relationship of residues of specific additives found in many foods.

Healthier replacement~ Chicory (imitation coffee.) Or Black Strap Molasses

Fast foods~ Sold commercially, or made at home, when inspected by the FDA, frankfurters (both beef and the beef-pork varieties) revealed more than one hundred and twenty different pesticide residues, including more than a dozen pesticide formulas. Those samples studies by the FDA had more than seven pesticides (a quarter of all samples) which were found to be; Dieldrin, Heptachlor, BHC, HCB, Lindane, DDT, Octachlor, and Penta.

Other pesticide chemicals found less often was: Diazinon, Malathion, Tecnazene, Chlorpyrifos and Toxaphene. Over one million Americans regularly eat hot dogs, and that translates into meaning that there are as many as a couple dozen types of "**carcinogens**" present in at least one million individuals at any given moment. That equation means that we can expect more than a thousand newly diagnosed cases of Cancer annually. And hot dogs contain nearly five grams of fat, along with a couple dozen milligrams of cholesterol.

Bologna~ The FDA (Food And Drug Administration) did a study on bologna, and more than a quarter of the samples used revealed more than one hundred pesticide residues, indicating a presence of nine pesticide formulations. Those toxins included: DDT, Dieldrin, Heptachlor, Lindane, HCB, BHC, and Penta. While the presence of PCB'S were not often found, they were found! *Along with these pesticide residues, two slices of bologna contains six grams of saturated fat, and more than thirty grams of cholesterol.* If you must feed bologna to your children, consider the less fatty types such as chicken, or turkey bologna. And vary their lunches so that they are not consuming bologna on a regular basis.

Bread ~ (refined white) ~ Whole grains, stone-ground or organically grown such as; Millet, corn flour, potato flour, spelt, rice, oat, soy or a combination of same.

Coffee replacements (healthier) ~ Chinese green tea (Oolong), Chicory which is an excellent tonic, laxative and diuretic.

Creams (whipped)~ Carnation skimmed can milk.

Butter ~ No-fat sour cream, almond butter, tahini, soy butter, organic rapeseed oil, or any other oil low in saturated fat.

Eggs ~ Egg whites, eggbeaters, silken tofu, or non-fat yogurt.

Fast food hamburgers~ The FDA'S "Total Diet Study" regarding fast food hamburgers included the lettuce, the buns, tomatoes, and also the condiments used on the hamburgers. Pesticide residues showed nearly one hundred and fifteen pesticide residues, resulting from fourteen pesticide formulations. Those pesticides pinpointed were; Chlorpyrifos, Diazinon, Dieldrin, HCB, DDT, Heptachlor, Lindane, Parathion, Endosulfan, BHC, Fenitrothion, Octachlor, Chlorpropham, and Penta. They also include seven grams of saturated fat, and seventy grams of cholesterol. Once the above facts are realized, it does not take too much persuasion to convince health conscious individuals to make healthier food selections.

Healthier replacements: Vegetable, or soy burgers.

Note: In the Resource chapter of this book we have provided Meat Manufacturers who ship frozen meats to customers such as beef and poultry. These animals are feed "Organic grains", and use no Nitrates, Nitrites, or Food Colorings in their products.

Juice~ Many Canned, or processed juices contain added sugars in the form of High fructose, or Acorn syrup. But the actual juice content is often lest than ten percent. Too, they contain food coloring, and other additives that trigger an allergic response in individual who are sensitive to these additives, and provide little, if any, nutritional value.

Healthier replacement~ Diluted unsweetened, one hundred

percent juice concentrate.

Milk~ While milk is definitely a good source for Calcium, it also often contains a fair supply of fat, and is often one of the food types most often associated with the development of Allergies. In the processing of milk, there are often Additives included, and the cumulative effect of chemical substances can be detrimental to individuals with an already weakened Immune System. For those individuals who have no allergies, and prefer the taste of milk, a one-percent fat content, or even Skim milk is just as nutritious as those milks with a higher fat content.

Healthier replacement~ Soymilk, or rice milk. For baking recipes, try powdered buttermilk.

Oil (cooking) ~ Virgin olive oil is preferred, but another alternative for sautéing is to replace oil with a low-sodium chicken broth, low sodium Soy sauce, or a light cooking wine.

Potatoes~ While potatoes eaten in moderation is acceptable, it is wise to remember that they are high in starch, but offer minimal nutrients. Mashed potatoes with butter and milk add calories, as does brown gravy. Fried potatoes become high in fat, and if bought at a Fast Food Restaurant are often fried in hydrogenated oils.

Healthier replacements~ At the Center for Science, studies were conducted a few years ago, in order to determine which vegetables were the most abundant in nutrients. It may surprise you to learn that Sweet potatoes won hands down. They contain the highest percent of Recommended Daily Allowances for Vitamins A and C, and for the Minerals Calcium, Copper, Folate and Iron. Second

Runner-Up was Carrots, followed closely by Collard greens, peppers, kale, dandelion, broccoli, and spinach. Wild, or Brown rice is a healthy choice, and can be alternated for the white potato. *Note: There is a delicious recipe for Cauliflower in the recipe section, and it is cooked in a way which makes it take on many of the characteristics of Sautéed potatoes.*

Raisins~ In FDA sampling studies, Raisins and Peanut butter ranked at the top of the list for pesticide residues. Sixteen samples of Raisins revealed one hundred and ten industrial and chemical residues, representing seventeen various formulations. Some of the toxins frequently making its presence known were as follows; Captan, Chlordane, Chlorpyrifos, Diazinon, Malathion, Nonachlor, Phosalone, Tributyl Phosphate, and Sulfur.

Healthier replacement~ Organically grown raisins are similar in cost to the commercial type, yet are shown to contain minimal, if any, pesticide residues. Too, Dole (a major supplier) of produce has decided to provide organic raisins, and have already purchased their own Packing factory. Purchasing organic raisins is highly recommended.

Refined white sugar ~ For hot drinks use the powdered herb Stevia. For baking, replace refined white sugar with strained baby foods such as; Prunes, peaches, applesauce. And another consideration depending upon recipe might be frozen concentrated white grape juice; without added sugar. Other natural sweeteners (which are better metabolized by the human body) include; Barley malt syrup, rice malt granules, and for special occasions, date sugar.

Salt (sodium chloride) ~ Sea salt, garlic, cayenne, cumin, dulse, kelp, oregano, or experiment with other favorite seasoning herbs.

Soft drinks~ These drinks often contain huge amounts of refined white sugar, food colorings, and other Additives. They also contain a fair share of Caffeine. The sugar contained in this type of beverage often interferes with the body's ability to store B+Complex vitamins, and these vitamins are necessary in order to maintain optimum health of the Central Nervous System, for the production of neurotransmitters, and for proper digestion, among other body functions. Individuals who are hypersensitive to food colorings, or have allergies, are often allergic to these soft drinks. They have no nutritional value, yet are high in calories, thus contributing to such disorders as; Diabetes, Obesity, High Blood Pressure, High Cholesterol, or possibly even Cancer.

Healthier replacements~ Unsweetened juice concentrates, twice diluted.

Tea, Black~ Black tea derives its color from the oxidation that occurs as a result of being heated at very high temperatures. These teas contain Caffeine, a substance that the FDA recommends further studying of, in order to determine whether or not, excessive consumption may have an association with the development of Cancer. It also contains Tannic Acid, an acid that is antagonistic with several of the body's internal processes, including its ability to manufacture and store specific Minerals, such as Iron.

Tea, Green~ This tea is the healthiest replacement for black tea. It undergoes a lesser heat treatment, and is therefore able to retain many of its compounds that have recently been found to be beneficial. One of those beneficial chemical constituents are its polyphenols, especially one in particular that is known as "Catechins." In Laboratory Studies, Catechins have been shown to exert a certain protection against free radicals. Some Experts believe that they accomplish this by enhancing the body's Immune System.

Water~ There is just about no better way of quenching one=s thirst than with pure, clear water. As humans, our total composition is made up of almost two-thirds water. Water assists the body in its effort to continually maintain the proper internal ph, and to flush toxins from the body. While fresh lemon is thought to be acidic, when it is added to water, and combined with the body's digestive juices, it not only becomes more of an alkaline, but it helps the body to maintain a proper ph. An internal environment that is too alkaline could contribute to possibility for the development of parasites. It is the Alkaline/Acidic ratio that keeps the internal environment healthy. As individuals begin to mature, the thirst signal is often not functioning as well as it once did, along with the sense of smell, hearing, and eyesight. This is exactly why many elderly individuals dehydrate in warmer climates. Though their body requires more water than they are drinking, they are not driven by thirst!

Note: *While there may have been a time when we believed that "water was water, those days are long gone! We have come a long way, but not all of it has been a positive experience. We have been victim to oil spills, chemical dumping in our Oceans, and roadside* *pesticide spraying. Using a good filter for the home water supply (such as Brita or Purr) is a wise investment, along with having the drinking water supply tested at a local Laboratory. Take your water Testing Results to your local Municipality, and compare your "Results" with their Area Chart List of "Safe Levels."*

Breads

White~(enriched) Flour being the main ingredient in the making of bread. White bread however, is made from "Enriched" white wheat flour. In other words, in the Milling of white wheat flour, its many nutrients are lost. Only minimal requirements of a mere few of the many placed using synthetic sources. The FDA (Food and Drug Administration) requires that riboflavin, niacin, thiamin, and iron be put back, making it an "Enriched" bread. Low in fiber, it is deficient in both copper and zinc, including many other of the B+ vitamins. Besides being low in many essential nutrients, these Supermarket variety of enriched white breads also contain many commonly used additives such as: Bleaching agents, Colorings, Dough Conditioners, Emulsifiers, Preservatives, Wheat gluten, and yeast.

Note: Due to the poor nutritional value of bleached, enriched flours, and their synthetic food colorings, additives and preservatives, many individuals with hyper sensitivities may experience a feeling of bloatedness and/or insufficient assimilation as a result of a lack of digestive enzymes. More information regarding deficiencies, including those associated with denatured foods can be found the chapter heading titled "Additives ."

Pumpernickel~ Usually made from a type of refined Rye, pumpernickel gets its dark color from adding caramel or molasses. It holds no advantage over white or rye breads.

Note: *Some Super Markets offer a small, square shaped, extra dark variety of packaged pumpernickel bread which is made from one hundred percent unbolted rye flour, and this variety does contain some of its original germ, and bran.*

Rye~ Because a bread made with one hundred percent rye flour would be very dense, yet offer very little Shelf-life due to its volatile germ, and bran content, it is not commonly made available. Consequently, most rye breads are actually a combination of rye, and wheat, or "Enriched Wheat" flour that has had its bran and germ removed. Select breads which are made from dark variety Ryes which may offer more "Rye" than some combinations.

Sprouted~ There are many versions of Sprouted breads, and they include: Alfalfa, bean sprouts, lentil, pea, mung, and soy. Sprouted breads add protein, and fiber that makes than filling, yet low in calories. They also lend a distinctive taste and flavor that is unique unto themselves.

Stone ground~ These grains are most regarded as nutritious because in the process of grinding, the grain is able to retain its nutrients because it is accomplished without using heat.

Note: *Because all of the grains nutrients are intact, these "Whole grains" should not only be kept refrigerated, but only purchased from a Supplier who has stored them in a freezer.*

Wheat~ There are several types of wheat flour. Bulgur (a type of cracked wheat), Farina that is milled to a fine consistency, and often used in making cereals, or pasta. There is a "Hard wheat" which contains more protein, such as Durum. Durum is the hardest variety of all wheat types, and is commonly processed into semolina that makes for a hearty pasta. There is also "Cracked wheat" and "Bulgur." Wheat contains a fair share of protein, and the usual amount of fat, but has absolutely no vitamin A, or vitamin content. Wheat contains gluten, a substance that is sticky and gelatinous, and often used by Pre-Schoolers with water (mixed to the right consistency) to form a paste that could be used as a glue. And it is because of its high gluten content that wheat is often associated with gastrointestinal problems. It has been identified as an allergen source for many individuals who are hypersensitive to gluten, or have a gluten intolerance. Pastry flour, or cake flour is wheat flour that has been processed in a way that removes some of its gluten. Breads labeled wheat are not necessarily made from "whole wheat." As a matter of fact, unless noted otherwise, most wheat breads are made from a combination of wheat and white flour, and with white flour comprising about seventy five percent of the total mixture. Enriched white flour is deficient in copper and Zinc, and most of the B+ Complex vitamins. It is also very low in fiber.

Note: Those who have a known intolerance to breads and flours that are high in gluten usually fare well with Spelt, or Kamut. These breads and flours are available at Health Food Stores.

Whole grains~ These are breads and flours which are made from the "Whole" grain, and have not been overly processed. Usually they contain more of their natural nutrients, and/or fiber.

Cereals (Packaged)

Many processed cereal packages are high in refined white sugars, and include additives such as artificial food colorings, and others. Yet they very often are low in fiber, and offer only minimal amounts of nutrients. In selecting a breakfast cereal that is low in sodium, refined . white sugar products, yet contains a good source of fiber and nutrients, consider one which is a Whole grain, such as rolled oats. Read the Ingredient label, and follow a guideline similar to the following: **Sodium;** Content should ideally be below 90 milligrams per 4 ounce serving. **Sugars:** An acceptable range per serving might be between 6 and 10 grams. **Fiber:** One gram, or less per serving might be considered unacceptable, look for a cereal type which provides a minimum of 2 grams of fiber, and ideally 3 to 4 grams per serving. Sweeten your cereal with fresh fruits, and kick up the taste with your favorite spice, such as Cinnamon. If the Ingredient label indicates several types of "Additives", such as food coloring dyes, another selection may be best for those individuals who are hypersensitive to these dyes.

Note; There is promise of a refined white sugar (processed) by the year 2000. It is said to be derived from the red beet, but will not undergo extensive processing.

Dairy Products

Butter~ High in fat, butter is made from milk products. Because it is a concentrated saturated fat that is associated with the development of raised blood cholesterol levels, and artery blockage, it should be either "Limited", or totally eliminated from the diet, depending upon such variables as: Age, life-style, health, and etc. Butter does contain some amount of the vitamins A, and

A healthier replacement for butter is as follows; For frying, or Sautéing, try Virgin olive oil, for baking, try using a spray for cupcake, and cake pans, as an ingredient for baking, substitute prunes. And for those special occasions when only butter will satisfy, try Ghee. Ghee is clarified butter, and can be acquired this way; After heating butter to nearly a boil, remove from heat, and allow to cool. When the butter has cooled sufficiently, scoop out the fat which has risen to the top, or surface of the butter. The remaining portion of butter is that portion which is low in fat, and is called Ghee.

Cheese~ This dairy product is made through a process whereby the curd is separated from the whey (or water portion) of the milk. Cheese is a good source of protein and Calcium, but is often high in saturated fat, Sodium, Cholesterol, and calories. Cheese contains no fiber.

Before offering any substitutes for cheese, and because the many available varieties vary greatly in their fat content, sodium, calories and etc., the following is a partial reference list.

The following numbers are based on 3-1/2 ounce Servings

	Fat	**Saturated**	**Calories**	**Sodium (mg.)**
Blue Cheese	29	19	353	1395
Brick	30	19	371	560

Brie	28	17	334	629
Cheddar	33	21	403	620
Colby	32	20	395	605
Cottage 1%	01	<	72	405
Cottage 2%	2	1	90	405
Cream	35	22	349	295
Feta	21	15	265	1116
Gouda	27	18	355	819
Gruyere	32	19	413	336
Limburger	27	17	325	800
Monterey	30	19	375	535
Mozzarella	17	11	280	528
Part skim				
Mozzarella	25	16	318	415
Whole milk				
Muenster	30	19	368	625
Parmesan	26	16	390	1600
Port Salut	28	17	350	535
Provolone	27	17	353	875
Ricotta-				
part skim	8	5	138	125
Ricotta-				
whole milk	13	8	175	85
Romano	27	17	385	1200
Roquefort	31	19	370	1800
Swiss	28	18	375	260

A healthier replacement for cheese might be either firm, or Silken Tofu. In fact, in the recipe section of this Cookbook, You will find a delicious recipe for a Cheesecake made by using The silken Tofu in place of cheese. Other choices for other Recipes could be; Goat cheese or fermented Tofu.

Note; *½ cup or ½ pound of tofu has the following nutritional profile;*

Protein	9.4 grams
Calcium	154.0 milligrams
Potassium	50.0 milligrams
Iron	2.0 milligrams
Fat	5.0 grams
Sodium	8.0 milligrams
Calories	86

Cream~ Very high in saturated fat, and calories, light cream contains about 700 calories per cup, and contains some cholesterol, and no fiber. Heavy cream contains over 800 calories per cup, and much more saturated fat.

A healthier replacement for cream might include: Condensed skim milk, or in a baking recipe, consider a no-fat, or low-fat Sour cream.

Eggs~ Egg whites, or any good egg substitute might help to limit the number of weekly eggs one consumes, but since eggs contain a natural source of lecithin (a substance which helps to escort LDL, or the "Bad cholesterol" out of the body, therefore, moderation is the key when eggs are the subject. Today many chickens are being raised and fed without meat by-products from animals, which will significantly reduce cholesterol ingested from eggs.

Ice cream~ Because ice cream often contains many food additives, or food dyes which are often associated with allergies in hyper-sensitive individuals, or if an individual is seeking to better manage his, or her weight, or cholesterol, they may want to eliminate ice cream all together. Ice cream raises triglyceride, and elevated triglyceride are often associated with heart attacks, or strokes. Ice cream in high in saturated fat, and high in calories.

A healthier replacement for ice cream; Consider a product found in most Health Food Stores which is made with Rice, hence "Rice Cream." Frozen fresh fruits, or frozen concentrated unsweetened fruit juice are healthier replacements for processed sugar, and will satisfy your Sweet-tooth cravings. Still there are others, including low fat Soy products. Check out the Freezer section of your local Health Food Store next time you are in the Market..

A more familiar replacement for Ice Cream is of course, the frozen yogurt.

See recipe for Ice cream using blanched Almonds and fruit.

Milk~ Milk is a good source of Calcium, and vitamin D. However, the same amount of Calcium, and vitamin content can be found in a milk with a lesser amount of fat. It is a good idea to move gradually from a 2 percent milk to a 1 percent milk, and then again to a skim milk. Making a gradual transition makes for a smoother change, and the taste buds will adapt without too much resistance. For those who are susceptible to Allergies, a milk made from rice might be preferable, or Goat's Milk

Dried Fruits

There are two basic varieties of dried fruits; Sulphured, and Unsulphured. Sulphured fruits have been sprayed with a chemical known as "Sulphur dioxide", before drying. Unsulphured, or "Sun-dried" fruits may be a better choice for some, but individuals who are sensitive to yeast, they should know that several of the Sun-dried fruits (such as raisins) contain a good amount of yeast.

Flour

Refined white~ Most Supermarket breads are made from a bleached white flour, and has been "Bleached" in order to speed up the maturing process, and to provide a more appealing visual look. And in order to lengthen the shelf-life of these breads, and other bakery products, most of the flours nutrients have been removed, and minimal amounts of a Synthetic vitamin is added in order to follow the FDA'S Guidelines. These breads contain little, or no fiber at all, and this is why they are so light in weight.

Unbleached white~ This type of white flour is similar to the above described white flour, except it has not been bleached. However, it still has had most of its nutrients removed, in order to lengthen its shelf life.

Organic unbleached white~ Organic unbleached implies that this type of flour has not been bleached, nor has its nutrients be removed. And no food additives have been incorporated into its compound. However because it is organic (alive), it must be refrigerated, in order to maintain freshness.

Note: *A product which carries the label "Certified Organic" means that the soil in which it has been grown does not use chemicals, and has passed the Government's Testing Standards, and that the soil shows no chemical, or pesticide residues above that which might minimally be"* Allowed."

Whole Grains ~ Flours made from whole grains are high in fiber, and a good source of complex carbohydrates. Most of the population today has insufficient fiber in their daily food-combining intake. To maintain satiety, control cholesterol levels, and protect the health of the colon, most Experts believe that 20 to 20 grams of daily fiber is most desirable. Whole grains include some of the following: Rice, Oats, Quinoa, corn, and wheat. Rice is a non-allergic grain, except for one variety, which is the sweet glutinous type. Oats are high in fat, but contain an antioxidant that delays rancidity. Quinoa is the only grain that is a complete source of protein.

Note: Whenever whole grains are served next to a legume, or with beans, they become a complete source of protein.

More Grains and Flours, not commonly used are;

Amaranth~ Amaranth flour contains twice as much protein as corn, but not near as much as Quinoa. It lends itself well for making crackers, and flatbread. If this is a flour one is just experimenting with, try using 1/3 of a cup to every cup of whole wheat a recipe calls for.

Arrowroot~ This flour is derived from the maranta plant, and is practically "All starch." It is very easily digested, and is often used in the making of biscuits, or crackers for children. It is as much a thickener as is cornstarch.

Barley~ An ideal flour for individuals following a gluten-free diet, Barley is rich in phosphorus, potassium, and sulfur. And it is thought that Barley stimulates the liver and the lymphatic system, aiding in the expelling of toxic waste from the body. Barley also contains *tocotrienol*, a substance that aids the suppression of cholesterol production in the liver.

Buckwheat~ Unrelated to the wheat family, Buckwheat is often an ingredient for making tasty pancakes. Buckwheat has the reputation of satisfying hunger for many hours, and is highly nutritious. Some of its nutrients include; Many of the B Complex vitamins, vitamin E, and its high source of Rutin can help strengthen the capillaries, thereby decreasing the risk of hemorrhages.

Bulgur wheat~ Sold in Health Food Stores, it is par-boiled, dried, and cracked. It is often found in cereals, pilafs, salads, and bakery products. It is rich in some of the B vitamins, including niacin and choline, along with a few minerals.

Corn~ Ground, it is commonly used for making cornbread. Given to us by the Indians, it becomes a source of complete protein when the Amino Acid Lysine is added.

Jerusalem Artichoke~ Providing a stronger texture, and flavor enhancement, it is often added to pasta flour (at one-tenth of the total mixture.) Diabetics can enjoy the benefits of this flour most perhaps, as it is a non-digestible carbohydrate that will not greatly affect blood sugar levels.

Oat~ Oat flour can either be milled from the whole oat, or from the kernel, or can be made at home by grinding the oat in a coffee grinder. Often added to commercial cereals, it is a good source of fiber.

Rye~ A favorite flour in the making of several varieties of bread. Light rye flours are often sifted to remove the bran and germ. Dark ryes usually still contain their bran and germ, thus providing more fiber.

Soy~ Obtained from the grinding of defatted soybeans, it is an excellent source of protein. And can be added to other flours in varying measures in place of another flour.

Other Organic an unprocessed Flours include;

These flours are not commonly found in the Supermarkets because they are usually "Unprocessed", therefore requiring refrigeration space in order to maintain freshness.

Kamut~ A distant relative to durum wheat, but with less gluten content, Kamut is generally better tolerated by individuals with a gluten intolerance, or other allergies. This flour is also more nutritionally fortified than wheat, and contains protein, magnesium, Zinc, and other minerals. Because its flavor is pleasant tasting, it lends itself well to most foods, including pasta.

Millet~ Said to be the oldest grain known, Millet goes back to Biblical times. Its nutritional profile is excellent: It contains more potassium than a banana, and stands beside Amaranth, Quinoa, and Soy as an excellent source of protein. It also contains choline iron, and lecithin. Millet is the only grain because it is alkaline, is good for maintaining the health of the pancreas, spleen, and stomach. *Experiments conducted at Yale University show that Millet has a more nutritious profile than does any other grain. That includes its unsaturated fat content, and it is a higher source of protein, minerals and vitamins.*

Spelt~ While its high fiber content assists in maintaining a healthy blood lipid (cholesterol, or fat) level, but because it is high in carbohydrates, it may not be the most suitable for Diabetics. Nutritionally, Spelt is abundant in many of the Amino Acids, protein, and B-Vitamins. This grain too, is a good replacement for wheat in individuals who are intolerant of gluten.

Wheat~ The substance which makes bread rise is known as "Gluten", a sticky nitrogenous compound which is most available in wheat. This sticky substance forms a mucus that layers the Villi, a part of the Intestines. However, should the Villi become too heavily covered by this tacky covering, nutrients are unable to be properly absorbed, and can result in a condition known as malabsorption. The average individual's diet is over abundant in wheat consumption, and is associated with many disorders. Clogging of the digestive system can lead to an impairment of the myelin sheath, the covering that normally protects the nerves. Those who already are experiencing digestive problems might fare well to consider alternating other flours into their diet, flours such as Barley, Millet, Oats, or Soy.

Note: There are other flours too, such as **Potato** flour that can be added to soups, gravies, stews, and breads to thicken, and to add taste.

Graham flour is obtained by grinding the kernel from the wheat known as "Winter Wheat." And the kernel's outside bran is left in its natural course and flaky state. A Doctor by the name of Graham who continually denounced white bread, calling it "Even less useless than useless.." Graham crackers were later named after him.

Almond meal that is derived from the Almond nut, and not from a grain, has been used successfully as a flour of sorts by grinding the nuts down into a course consistency. It is highly nutritious, pleasantly sweet tasting, low in fat, and low enough in carbohydrates that it can be useful as an ingredient in cooking for Diabetics, or those on carbohydrate, or refined white sugar products. *At back of book, find a list of Suppliers for ordering products.*

Almond Meal, or any other Meal, such as Corn Meal refers to a coarser texture derived through a quick blending, or special blade type used in the blending. A Flour is a smooth, fine powdery consistency, and Meal is a larger coarser texture.

Frozen Foods ~

Desserts~ Frozen fruits are often a good way to stock fruits for those times when they are out of Season. They can be used in a protein drink, heated as a pancake topping, or simply thawed and eaten. However; *"Read the Ingredient Labels carefully."* Those containing Sauces, or creams might very well be a source for added sugars, food colorings, and other sources of saturated fats, or sodium.

Entrees~ One of the first ingredients deserving mention with relation to frozen Entrees is that most of the Sodium content in these prepared, or processed meals usually ranges from 600 milligrams of Sodium to as high as 1200 milligrams of Sodium. Become educated regarding the potential toxicity, and/or safety regarding those food additives, and preservatives which are most often listed on Ingredient labels of the foods favored by your family members. Whenever possible, fresh foods, or whole foods are always best!

Vegetables~ Frozen vegetables may be a convenient way to take advantage of your Freezer, and its ability to store a variety of fresh vegetables, without the usual required time it takes to peel, grate, or chop. As with frozen fruits, always select those varieties that have only natural ingredients, low sodium, low sugar (preferably none), and low fat content. Be aware that many creamed vegetables, or vegetables in Sauces may contain Allergy-triggering additives.

Note: Cascadian Farm in Rockport, MA. 98283 at www.cfarm.com, or at 719 Metcalf Street, Sedro-Woolley, WA. 98284 is a good source for packaged frozen meals. For instance; "Organic Moroccan Vegetarian Meal" combines Bulgur wheat, Lentils, Garbanzo Beans, Vegetables and Raisins with exotic North African Seasonings in a one-pound package in the frozen food section. They also offer several other tasty versions of One-dish Entrees, and most are low in fat (no saturated fat), and high in fiber. Read labels, and be conscious of Sodium content, and calories as they pertain to individual portions. The Moroccan Organic Vegetable Meal contains no food additives, food colorings, or hydrogenated oils, and are therefore, a healthy selection when time is of the essence.

Irradiation of Vegetables (and fruits)~ Irradiation of food has been surrounded by much contraversary. At this point, Manufacturer's who utilize this process as a way to kill organisms that damage food, or cause human illnesses, are supposed to label these foods so that Shoppers can make their own choice regarding this spoil control processing. Irradiation takes "Processing" to a higher level, using famma radiation from radioactive cobalt or cesium, among viable sources of X-rays. Foods that are most likely to be processed using Irradiation include; Produce, including Strawberries, and potatoes, but other foods which spoil rapidly such as Poultry, pork and seafood are also being inducted into the new processing technique. This information was offered in 1992 by the University of California at Berkley Wellness Letter. Those who object to Irradiating food contend that it is still uncertain whether or not this process poses a threat to human health, and point to the fact that this process has no way of proving that it will not negatively effect the environment.

Luncheon Meats ~ Luncheon meats such as Bologna, Salami, Ham, and similar types of processed meats contain added Colorings, and high amounts of Sodium Chloride (table salt) which can adversely effect blood pressure in some individuals, raising it to dangerous levels. Luncheon meats also often contain other additives, and preservatives that can trigger an allergic response in individuals who are susceptible. They also contain preservatives known as Nitrites, and Nitrates. When combined with the

Stomach's natural digestive juices, they begin to form a substance called "Nitrosamines" which are known carcinogens. These meats should be limited, and a Vitamin -C supplement of 1,000 milligrams taken at the same time that one consumes foods containing these chemicals, will help to inhibit their formation.

Note: Healthier replacements~ Fresh tuna Salad (packed in water), homemade egg Salad, Vegetable cheeses made from Soy products, home-made Soups, or sandwiches made from leftover oven roasts.

NUTS

Almonds~ While many nuts are high in nutrition, they should be consumed in moderation due to their high fat content. Some however, are very low in their "Saturated fat" content, and contain many other essential minerals. Almonds contain a substance known as "Laetrile" which has been identified by Scientists as a "Cancer fighting agent." They is also abundant in phosphorus, potassium, protein and magnesium. They are often said by many food experts to be the best choice for nuts. Two ounces of Almonds contain 30 grams of fat (only 2 saturated), and zero cholesterol.

Note; Almonds and Chestnuts, including Cashews can be made into a healthier form of butter than the traditional animal type, recipes can be found in chapter titled "How to prepare healthier food Alternatives for traditional High-fat Ingredients.

Cashews~ A good source of vitamin-A, magnesium, and a few other minerals, Cashews are also high in fat. Two ounces of Cashew nuts contain 26 grams of fat (Six saturated), and zero cholesterol.

Chestnuts~ Roasted Chestnuts contain less fat than any other type of nut. *Two ounces contain two grams of fat (Zero saturated), and no cholesterol.*

Hazelnuts~ Filberts, or Hazelnuts are very mild in flavor, therefore lend themselves well to a variety of dishes. A good source for Calcium, potassium, and sulphur. Two ounces of Hazelnuts contain approximately thirty-five grams of fat (Two of which are saturated), and zero cholesterol.

Macadamia~ Very high in fat, a two ounce roasted portion contains nearly 45 grams of fat, but only four are of the saturated type. They contain no cholesterol, but are high in calories. On the up side, they do provide a good source of iron, magnesium, and thiamin.

Peanuts~ High in fat, these nuts also contain a carcinogen known as aflatoxin. Peanuts however, are not nuts, but belong to the family of Legumes. A two ounce serving of peanuts contain 28 grams of fat, 4 of those fat grams are saturated. Peanut butter is higher in fat than roasted peanuts.

Pecans~ Abundant in essential fats, Pecans are relatives of the Hickory family. A two-ounce serving contains thirty-eight grams of fat, four of which are saturated fats.

Pistachios~ Mild, yet flavorful, these nuts are said to owe their distinct taste to a minute worm which leaves tiny holes in the nuts. A two-ounce serving of Pistachios contain nearly thirty grams of fat, four of which are saturated.

Sesame seeds~ Available either hulled, or unhulled, the latter type has a deeper color, and still has the bran in tact. They provide several essential minerals, including iron, calcium, and phosphorus. The Calcium however, is unable to be utilized by the human body because it is bound by oxalate. Sesame seeds are relatively low in fat, and a two-ounce serving contains only eight grams of fat, two of which are saturated.

Sunflower seeds~ While there are a few types of Sunflower seeds, they are teardrop shaped and come from a gray, or white colored shell. However, there is another type that is the oil sunflower that is held in a black shell. Abundant in many minerals, such as Calcium, folacin, vitamin B-6, and thiamin, they are also higher in calories and fat. A two-ounce serving contains twenty-eight grams of fat, four are of the saturated variety.

Walnuts~ A popular nut used in many recipes, Walnuts are a good source of protein, magnesium, potassium, and vitamin-A. A two-ounce serving contains thirty-two grams of fat, four of them saturated.

***Note*:** *For a healthier selection, whenever possible choose unsalted, or lightly salted nuts.*

For individuals interested in pursuing a Vegetarian Life-style, nuts provide a good source of protein.

Prepared or Processed Foods

A prepared, or processed food is a food which is often found in either a box, a bag, or a can. And in order to prevent contamination, specific Additives and Preservatives are used in the manufacturing

process. In the process to preserve the particular food and its shelf life, nutrients are often removed, and other synthetic minimal nutrients are replaced in accordance with the FDA'S requirements. While many "Additives" are safe, if not beneficial, it is important to familiarize one's self with each category, or class.
Note: The first Chapter of this book is dedicated to Additives, and Preservatives, most of which could lead to a potential health threat when consumed in excess. For more information regarding food additives, and food preservatives (including those which are safe), look for "FOOD ADDITIVES, NUTRIENTS AND SUPPLEMENTS A TO Z" by Clear light Publishers, or Call 1-800-253-2747 to Order, or On-line visit www.NaturalHealingDr.com.
A healthier replacement for prepared foods (those most commercialized, such as those most often found in a box, bag, or a can) that are Additive and Preservative free (and it is common knowledge that these Additives and Preservatives often trigger an Allergic response in hypersensitive individuals) are fresh foods; fresh fruits, fresh vegetable, nuts and grains, whenever possible.

OILS

Essential Fatty Acids~ Better known as the Unsaturated fatty acids, or Linoleic and Linolenic acids, or Omega 3 fatty acids. These nutrients are referred to as essential because though the human body cannot manufacture the essential fatty acid linoleic; the other two fatty acids "Archidonic" and "Linolenic" can be produced when sufficient amounts of linoleic acid is available, or present in the body. And while there are other sources for the Omega 3, or the

Omega 6 fatty acids, there is one good source available which contains both; Flax oil. The benefits provided by the Essential Fatty Acids include; An excellent source of energy (and Experts contend that about eighty percent of the population consumes inadequate amounts of these acids, and are therefore, deficient. The Essential Fatty Acids also are necessary components in all of the human body's nerve cells, cell membranes, and for the stimulation of hormone-like substances called Prostaglandin's. Experts tell us about sixteen prostaglandin's with various capabilities which include; Constricting and/or dilation of the blood vessels, uterine stimulation (used to induce birthing labor), stimulation of bronchial or intestinal smooth muscle, and effecting the body's efficiency at metabolizing of fats. In fact, nothing less than a book can provide the comprehensive data, which has been learned, and is available (all of it positive) regarding these Essential Fatty Acids, and how Flax oil is considered the highest purest form of these Fatty Acids.

Hydrogenated oils~ Manufacturers begin with a good unsaturated oil, and heat it at extreme temperatures (known as the process of hydrogenation), thereby breaking down the unsaturated oils molecular structure, converting them into harmful saturated fats, of the type which many Nutritional Experts believe, are carcinogens, raising one's risk of cancer.

Monosaturated from plant sources, and not contained in red meats, monosaturated fats, or oils do not affect blood lipid levels. The following are types of fats from which monounsaturated oils are made: Almonds, Apricot, Avocado, Canola, Cashews, Hazelnuts,

Olive oil, Peanut and Pecans.

Polyunsaturated oils~ These types of oils (or fats) are of liquid consistency, and are never converted into solid form. However, whenever these oils are "over-processed", much of their original health benefits are destroyed.

Saturated oils (fats)~ Left at room temperature, these fats will begin to solidify. Coconut, and Palm kernel are examples of saturated fats, but these two in particular, contain a substance known as lauric acid which is linked to clogged arteries. Butter, many Vegetable oils, lard, and Palm oil are other forms of saturated fats. Saturated fats are found in Beef, Poultry (the Skin), Chocolate, Milk and Cream, Processed cheeses, Bacon, and Pork.

Trans Fatty Acids~ These acids are formed through a type of processing which adds hydrogen molecules to natural fatty acids, converting them into "Unnatural Trans Fatty Acids." Trans fatty acids and hydrogenated oils interfere with the body's ability to store the much needed "Essential Fatty Acids." They are also associated with a higher risk of Cancer in individuals who regularly consume these harmful substances, or foods which contain them. Other disorders linked to Trans Fatty Acids include: Diabetes, Obesity, High Blood Lipid (Cholesterol) levels, and weakened Immune Systems.

Note: *Chemicals, pesticides, and herbicides are stored in the fatty tissues of animals. Those individuals who continually consume red meat, and dairy products are vulnerable to the accumulative effect of toxins. To assist the body in its attempt to prevent free radical* *injury to normal cells resulting from ingestion of rancid fats, and oils, supplement with Vitamin-E daily (400 I.U., or International Units.)*

Unsaturated oils~ To quotes the World renown European Biochemist who was nominated seven (7) times for her research and work regarding fats, Dr. Johanna Budwig relates: "The Americans finally understand the dangers associated with the saturated fats, but they still do not understand the benefits associated with the unsaturated fats, the Linolenic and the Linoleic Acids." Unsaturated fats include the following: Almond, Avocado, Canola, Flax, Olive, Rice bran (excellent for lowering high cholesterol levels) oil, Safflower, Sesame, and Walnut oils.

Note: *Dr. Budwig explains in her writings how an unsaturated oil is rated, or graded, which is accomplished according to each oils number of bonding chains, and molecular structure. And Dr. Budwig tells us that the highest, purest form of the Essential Fatty Acids (unsaturated fats) is Organic Flax Oil.*

Smoked Meats ~ See information under heading Luncheon meats. Meats that have been cured with nitrates, or nitrites form a chemical compound known as "Nitrosamines" when they are introduced to the body's digestive juices within the intestinal tract, and these nitrosamines are known to be potent carcinogens. It is wise to limit the amount of consumption of foods containing nitrites, and nitrates.

Jams and Jellies~ Choose only those brands which are made from "All fruit", and have no extra sugar added.

Peanuts~ High in fat, and calories, peanuts also contain a harmful substance known as aflatoxins, a known carcinogen.

Pop Corn~ Avoid the commercial, or healthier type, as they are high in fat, Sodium, and often contain artificial additives. Using the microwave, or an Air-popper designed for making popcorn, opt for lemon and pepper, or other favorite herbs for a healthier treat.

Potato Chips~ This type of Snack food contains little, if any, nutrients. But, they do contain additives, high Sodium Chloride (Table Salt) content, Colorings, preservatives, and etc.

Purchase a low Sodium, low fat chip that is "Baked", rather than fried.

Note: Some Health Experts now believe a possibility may exist between hyperactive children, and excessive Sodium Chloride intake. Excessive iodine consumption (as contained in many of these Snack food types) may “Over-stimulate” the Thyroid Glands.

Pretzels~ Lower in fat than many Snack Foods, pretzels often provide a small amount of added fiber to the diet. However, whenever possible choose varieties that are lower in Sodium, and without a long string of Colorings, and etc. There are a couple of types which are made from "Whole grains", and these may be a healthier choice.

CHAPTER THREE

How To Incorporate Healthier Food Choices As Replacements For Traditional Devitalized Favorites, And Why These Choices Are Health-Smart Decisions.

Dry Ingredients

Baking Powder~ Non-Aluminum type found in Health Food Stores.

Bleached white flour Unbleached white flour, (organic, or non-organic), Soy flour, Millet flour, Spelt, Kamut, Oat, Buckwheat, Maize, or Rice flour.

Flour (Refined White)~ Unbleached white (preferably organic), Corn Maize, Millet, Buckwheat, Oat, Rice, or Soy.

Pie Crust~ A no-fat graham cracker can lend itself well as a piecrust. Simply chop in the Blender, or mash in a deep bowl by hand.

Salt (Sodium Chloride)~Sea Salt (Dulse, Kelp), or Lemon & pepper, or other available blends of Spices. Brand Name products include the following; "Saltless" a registered Trademark by McCormick, “Mrs. Dash" a registered Trademark of Alberto-Culver, "No Salt" a registered Trademark by RCN Products, and "Seasoning" a registered Trademark by Bernard Jensen.

Refined white rice~ Brown rice, Wild rice, Jasmine rice.

Refined white sugar~ Date Sugar, Rice Malt Syrup, Barley Malt granules, Raisins, fresh fruits, frozen concentrated, unsweetened white grape juice, unsweetened Applesauce, strained baby foods, such as; Bananas, Prunes, Peaches and Applesauce. And there is *Sucanat,* an organically grown sweetener, it is evaporated can juice, often referred to as raw sugar. It is much healthier than bleached white sugar because nothing has been added, and only the water has been extracted. Therefore, all of its natural nutrients remain in tact.

Note: At Georgetown University, Researchers learned through Laboratory experiments using animals, that refined white Sugar was just as likely to raise blood pressure as was Sodium Chloride (Table Salt.) High fiber foods such as fresh fruits, or whole grains help to control abnormal cravings for sugar. The higher the daily intake of refined sugar, the greater the need for B+ Complex vitamins

Wet Ingredients

Butter~ Almond, or Soy butter are ideal alternatives. Ghee (clarified butter), or Silken tofu may be viable replacements for some recipes.

Another healthy replacement for butter is Lecithin, or a spread made from a liquid Soy Lecithin, unhydrogenated soybean oil, and beta-carotene.

Note; For those interested in preparing their own Almond, or Cashew butter, or other difficult to find products, refer to chapter titled Recipes on How To Incorporate Healthier Alternatives for Oils, and butter.

Almond Butter~ Most Super Markets sell a product known as "Almond Paste", but read the Ingredient label to be certain there is no extra Sugar added. Almonds are naturally sweet, yet so mild tasting that they do not over power the taste of foods that contain them. While Almond Butter can be purchased at most Health Food Stores, it can also be made at home in order to insure freshness.

Directions: Blanch one cup of shelled Almonds (leaving the Skins in tact, if desired.) Grind blanched Almonds in a Coffee Grinder, or Blender until they are of a powdery texture. Add a little water at a time to reach the preferred consistency.

Almond Cream~ Slightly different in taste, and texture to Almond Butter, Almond Cream lends itself well for making Icing, or Toppings for Baked goods such as desserts.

Directions; In a Blender, or Food Processor, mix the following Ingredients:

~ One cup of Almond butter (blanched Almonds)
~ One half of a Lemon, including grated rind
~ One cup of Unsweetened Apple juice, or Unsweetened frozen concentrated white grape juice.
~ One cup of silken tofu
~ After blending, chill in refrigerator

Cashew Butter~ Purchase fresh raw (preferably organically grown Cashews).

Directions; ~In a Blender, or Coffee Grinder, mix one cup of raw Cashews until they are converted into a fine powdery texture. Slowly incorporate a small amount of water gradually, until it has reached a smooth pasty consistency.

Chestnut Butter~ Soak two cups of dried Chestnuts for twelve to fifteen hours.

Directions; ~Place in a small pot, and cover with water, heat to a simmer.

~ Cook for approximately thirty-five to forty-five minutes.

~ Without any cooling, mix in a Blender, or Food Processor, along with Six cups of water.

Chestnut Cream~ Using two cups of Chestnut Butter, (Recipe provided),

Blend or Mix the following Ingredients;

Directions; ~ Two cups of Chestnut Butter (or dried Chestnuts, and follow Instructions for making Chestnut Butter.

~ Six cups of water

~ One teaspoon of cinnamon

~ One cup of unsweetened Apple juice (or unsweetened white grape frozen concentrate.

~ One teaspoon of pure Vanilla Extract.

~ Three tablespoons of pure maple syrup. (See Resource Chapter for sugar-free brands.)

Fruit pureed ~ Seeding, blending and straining of a fruit, or combination of fruits.

Chocolate~ Carob powder, or chips, Cocoa.

Cream~ No-fat Sour cream, condensed Skim milk,

Powdered Buttermilk Mix.

Eggs~ Egg whites, Rice Malt Syrup, Tofu, Egg Substitute.

Maple Syrup ~ Whenever a recipe calls for Maple Syrup, replace with Black Strap Molasses. It contains many essential Minerals and vitamins, including, iron, phosphorous, and B+ Complex vitamins.

See Steels (Product Manufacturer) in the Resource Chapter of this book for Sugar-free products, without raising risk of Cancer.

Note: *There will be several Resources listed on the back pages of this book for natural, chemical-free products.*

Milk~ Skim milk, Soymilk and Rice milk, including Goat=s milk.

Oil~ Rice Malt Syrup. Lecithin, and another healthier replacement for oil, and one that adds moisture, without the fat is Prunes. Pureed Prunes are high in sorbitol, a substance which attracts moisture.

Pancake Syrup~ Sliced Bananas, orange juice, cinnamon and Vanilla extract heated to just prior to the Boiling point is a healthy and naturally sweet alternative to Maple syrup which is usually highly processed..

To Sum Up ~ The following foods are best eliminated, or greatly reduced:

Bacon	Duck	Mayonnaise
Black olives	Egg yolks	Organ meats
Bologna	Palm kernel oil	Fried foods

Peanuts	Butter	Gravies
Poultry skin	Cheese, soft	Hamburger
Salami	Chocolate	Hot dogs
Sausages	Corned beef	Hydrogenated oils
Shelled fish	Coconut oil	Ice Cream
Smoked meats	Cream	Liver Sausage
Whole milk	Creamy dressings	Lunch meats

Canned and packaged products are often found to contain food Colorings, food additives, and preservatives, hydrogenated oils, high sodium content, and are basically unhealthy, and are often foods which can best be prepared at home. Foods best prepared at home include; Organ meats, dessert products, and Bakery products. Cereals and crackers should also be carefully chosen. Those of lower sodium and fat content are ideal.

CHAPTER FOUR

RECIPES

Many of the following recipes do not contain specific counts for; Calories, carbohydrates, fiber, fat or sodium. That is because these recipes are not necessarily provided as best choices for those individuals who are seeking to lose weight, diabetics, or those who must follow a sodium restricted diet.

Those individuals however, can make such adjustments to recipes contained herein. These recipes are offered only as examples of how each of us can eat healthier, and without overloading the body with chemicals contained in many prepared, and/or processed foods. These recipes point the way to how we can enjoy baked goods, without the bleached white flour, high gluten content (an allergy trigger for many hypersensitive individuals) often found in most flours in the Super Market today. Flours which often Advertise Semolina, or Oat will list wheat as the first ingredient on the ingredient label.

Diabetics could learn how to substitute healthier sweeteners that are better tolerated by their body (such as natural sweeteners made from fruit) due to their gradual effect upon the body's Insulin. Other suggestions will be found throughout this Holistic CookBook, such as the nutritious Rice Malt syrup, or Barley malt granules.

Should weight loss be one's goal, my professional opinion is that this too, can be achieved in part, through making healthier food choices, and by taking in fewer calories while expending more, exercise!

However, eating an abundance of low calorie denatured foods, rather than eating a moderate amount of nutritiously selected foods can be defeative, as it is a Trade-off and a compromise to good health. An Internal environment which is in tune, or is in balance with most of the essential nutrients and minerals will actually provide the best maintenance insurance for a good metabolism!

Note: When replacing whole grain, unbleached, and organic flours, much of the bloating experienced after eating foods made from bleached white fours (with food Colorings, preservatives and additives) will be eliminated. However, whenever a fat ingredient such as butter, or oil is called for in a traditional recipe, and is replaced with a healthier non-fat ingredient such as a fruit puree derived from plums and apples, or bananas, the final product (cake, muffin, and especially cookie) will become softer and moister, but will not be as "Short" a dough as we may have come to expect from foods high in fat. And for that very reason, it is important to fully cook each oven baked recipe, and to ensure that flour measurements are exact, otherwise your baked goodies may be softer and moister than desired. For those individuals who choose not to make a full transition from fat and sugar recipes to those which are no-fat, or sugar foods may be able to reach a happy medium through cutting the amount of fruit puree and/or brown rice syrup in half, and replacing the other half with olive oil. Because most of us have individual preferences and needs, the recipes contained herein are offered as a matter of demonstrating healthier choices, inspiring creativity, and implanting the idea how fats and sugars can be eliminated, especially for those who live with Diabetes, Obesity, CHD (Cardiovascular Heart Disease), and other health problems. With an open mind, we are able to change our taste, as many tastes are acquired.

Note: Many of the following recipes have been "Converted" into healthier recipes by substituting Organic flours, natural sweeteners, healthier oils, and etc. however, many of the following recipes ***have not*** *been converted.* Therefore, we suggest that you take those recipes that have not been converted into healthier recipes, and begin to substitute many of the "traditional" ingredients with the healthier substitutions we have provided for you in earlier Chapters.

BREAKFAST AND/OR DESSERTS

King's delight

Ingredients

1 2 pounds of the darkest seedless grapes (thoroughly rinsed)

1/4 teaspoon of cinnamon

1/4 cup of pecans or walnuts (unsalted, or lightly salted)

basic flatbread (either home made or prepared_

juice of 2 squeezed fresh lemon

Directions

Wash grapes and arrange neatly on simple flatbread and place on cookie sheet or pizza pan lightly sprayed with vegetable oil

Cut, and squeeze lemon juice over grapes

Sprinkle with cinnamon

Place cookie sheet (or pizza pan) in a preheated 350 degree oven for approximately 20 minutes.

Remove from oven and sprinkle with nuts, return to oven once again until grapes have burst and are bubbling.

Allow to cool before slicing.

Mmmmm good!.

****

L'Natural pancakes

Follow your everyday pancake recipe, except;
Replace bleached white flour with a combination of whole grain Flours, or you can now purchase HODGSON MILL blended whole grain flours at your local Food Market.

Our favorite is Buckwheat pancake mix that is a combination of Buckwheat, and whole-wheat flour. It is a stone ground whole grain flour and is available at most Super Markets.

1/3 cup of dry flour contains 3 whole grams of fiber.

Keep in mind that our body requires anywhere from 15 to 25 grams per day.

Replace traditional butter and/or Maple syrup which is mostly processed mostly sugar) ~

In a small fry pan add the following;

1/4 cup of dry walnuts halved

One sliced banana

* Optional; Dash of Cinnamon (and/or Vanilla Extract)

1/4 cup of orange juice

heat until boiling point and quickly turn off. Let rest for one minute and then use over pancakes.

****

BEVERAGES

Chinese Oolong Green Tea

Consider adding your favorite Extract, such as; Rum, Vanilla, Chocolate, Lemon, or Mint to your green tea.

Keep in mind that many of these delightful Herbal teas can be combined together to create that special tea which is tasty, and beneficial!

**Optional; Add ½ teaspoon of unprocessed brown sugar*

Note:

Oolong green tea contains polyphenols, one of which is "Catechins", has been shown in several Clinical studies, to boost the Immune system.

****

Sunshine Citrus Punch

Ingredients

1- 12-ounce can of frozen pineapple-orange juice

1-litter bottle of carbonated water (chilled)

1-Tablespoon of Lemon extract

1-12 ounce bottle of ginger ale.

Orange slice

Directions

In a small Punch bowl, combine thawed pineapple-orange juice concentrate, and lemon extract.

Gradually add chilled water, and then ginger ale to punch bowl, using gentle downward, and upward strokes.

Finally, add orange slices and allow to float.

Makes about 6- 10 ounce Servings..

****

LUNCHES AND/OR SNACKS

Diabetes friendly recipe

Ingredients

4 slices of whole grain bread

2 tablespoons unsweetened crushed pineapple

1 ripe banana

1/4 to 2 tsp. Of cinnamon

Spread the pineapple on 2 slices of bread.

Cover the pineapple with the banana strips, sprinkle each banana with cinnamon, cover with remaining two slices of bread.

Spray a fry pan with Pam and heat sandwich until lightly browned.

Recipe contribution by Grace Hesson

****

Chick Peas (Garbanzos)

Cayenne Roasted Garbanzo's

A moderate protein, low-fat snack

Ingredients

1 15-1/2 ounce can of Chick peas (also known as Garbanzo beans)

1 Tablespoonful of Extra virgin Olive oil

*Optional: Cayenne pepper

Directions

Pre-heat oven to 325 degrees

Place Chick peas into oven safe dish

Add Olive oil

Sprinkle with Cayenne or any other Seasoning of your choice such as;   Garlic, Nutmeg, or Crushed dill.

Bake for approx. 20 to 25 minutes or until Chick peas turn a light brown.

Makes three servings, each serving contains;   110 Calories-7 grams of protein and 7 grams of fiber.

Note: Cayenne can be substituted for any other preferred Seasoning as Garbanzo's are very bland and will take on the taste of most any seasoning or herb.

****

Iced Chinese Green Tea (Oolong)

Ingredients

In a large cooking pot add 5 cups of water

5 green tea bags

2- tablespoons of Raw or unprocessed sugar

Lemon extract*

1 tray of ice cubes

Bring tea bags to a full boil, quickly lowering heat to a minimum simmer. Cook for 5 minutes before turning heat off. Let stand for 5 minutes before adding remaining ingredients.

Strain tea prior to adding last ingredients to prevent any loose tea leaves from remaining in solution.

*Fresh lemon or vanilla, or peppermint extract may be substituted

*Fresh fruit may also be added for diversity

Note: *Chinese Oolong green tea contains polyphenols, And more specifically "Catechins" is one which has been Shown to contain remarkable anti-cancer abilities in Several Research Studies.*

Chinese green tea can be blended with any other of your Favorite herbal teas.

****

PITA PEPPERS

Ingredients

1- Fresh stalk of celery

1-Small Vidalia onion

Either/or all; Red roasted peppers, jalapeno peppers,

carrot shavings, sunflower seeds, tomato, onion, lettuce and

allow your imagination flow.

Shredded cheese; Jack, Mozzarella, American (preferably

low-sodium varieties)

Lite Soy sauce

Directions

In a small Sauté pan, add one spray of vegetable oil

Add onion at medium high heat, gradually adding other ingredients, including Lite Soy sauce and water as necessary.

Continue to cook on low heat until vegetables begin to turn soft (do not overcook)

Meanwhile on a cookie sheet, place pitas in a warm oven for a couple of minutes, as warm pitas are opened easier, without tearing.

Halved pitas are ideal.

When pitas are warmed at 300 degrees for a couple of minutes, turn oven off and begin to fill pita halves with sautéed veggies.

Sprinkle with low-fat cheese.

Low fat, low sodium and nutritious!

ENTREES

Catfish Almond

Ingredients

2 cup of plain dry bread crumbs

2 cup of whole natural Almonds

1 Tablespoon of Thyme

1 Tablespoon of dried chives

2 Teaspoon of Sea Salt

2 tsp. White pepper

1 Tablespoon of grated Lemon zest

3/4 to 1 cup of unbleached white all-purpose flour (organic preferred)

2 whole eggs lightly beaten (or equivalent egg substitute)

3 Tablespoons of Olive oil

*optional B 2 Tablespoons of Light butter

4 catfish fillets (about a pound and a half)

Directions

After grinding Almonds to a powdery consistency in a coffee grinder, place in a bowl together with bread crumbs, salt, pepper, chives, lemon zest and mix.

Transfer ground Almonds and bread crumbs to a plate

Flour each side of the catfish fillets, dip into egg mixture

Then coat each side of catfish with Almond batter and set aside on wax paper or a paper plate

Selecting a large nonstick skillet, heat oil (and optional butter) over medium heat.

Adding two fillets at a time, cook until browned, turning only once

When done, fish will flake easily when touched with fork

(Fish will be done when cooked approximately 4 minutes on each side)

Transfer to serving dish and keep warm

Repeat procedure by cooking remaining fillets

****This dish is complimented by serving side dish of Hush puppies (see recipe)***

Each serving contains about 505 Calories, 25 grams of fat, 40 grams of protein, 216 milligrams of cholesterol, 790 grams of sodium, 30 grams of carbohydrate, and 3 grams of fiber.

****

Crabby Crisps

Homemade Crab Cakes

Ingredients

1 pound of fresh crab fin

1/4 tsp. Cayenne pepper

4 tablespoons of prepared cracker meal

1 tablespoon of horseradish

1 tablespoon of low-fat (or no fat) mayonnaise

1 tsp. Of dry mustard

1/4 cup (or a bit less) of Lite cream

paprika (pinch)

Directions

Rinse crab, drain well and set aside

In a medium size mixing bowl add all ingredients (other than crab) and mix together.

Note: Adding only half of cream now and whatever needed later when crab is combined;

Add crab

Consistency should be wet, but not dripping when held in hand

Fill Six appetizer dishes with crab mixture

Sprinkle with paprika

*Optional ~ Add a touch of Light butter in order to lightly brown tops of mixture

*Dishes must be oven proof!

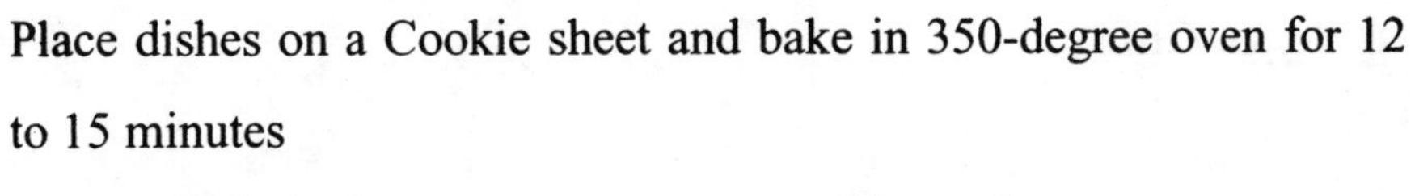

Place dishes on a Cookie sheet and bake in 350-degree oven for 12 to 15 minutes

Serve with baked potato or sweet potato fries and greens.

****

Chicken Chili

Ingredients

Two large boned skinless chicken breasts

Two (2) 26 ounce jars of Paul Newman=s Pasta Sauce (No additives, all natural)

Precooked or canned red kidney beans, equal to 2 to 2-1/2 cups *

Cayenne pepper

Chili powder to taste

One Bay leaf

Fresh grated mozzarella and/or Parmesan cheese

Directions

Into a large pot add the two jars of pasta sauce and heat at medium heat

Clean, trim chicken breasts and add to pasta sauce

Add Bay leaf

Salt to taste

Cayenne and Chili pepper to taste

Allow chicken to cook in sauce on medium heat for about 30 minutes stirring often, and until chicken begins to fall apart

Add kidney beans and continue to cook on low to medium flame

Adjust cayenne pepper and chili powder to taste

*1-Tablespoon of Olive oil (optional)

Serve over a bed of cooked rice and top with fresh grated cheese

A side of salad completes meal

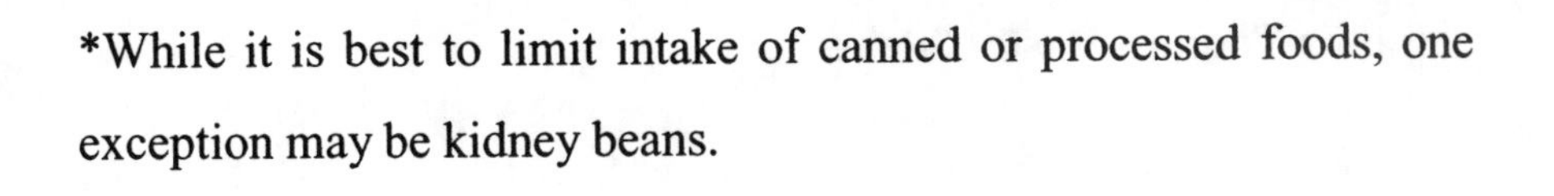
*While it is best to limit intake of canned or processed foods, one exception may be kidney beans.

****

Linda's Tomato-Basil Chicken

Ingredients

1 pound of boneless, skinless chicken breast (sliced thin)

2 teaspoons of Light butter divided

2 cup finely chopped shallots, leeks or onion

4 medium ripe plum tomatoes chopped

1/3 cup of white wine

3 tablespoons of fresh basil leaves chopped coarsely or 1 tablespoon of dried basil

2 cup of reduced fat sour cream or nonfat sour cream substitute

Salt and pepper to taste

*Optional (1/4 cup of slithered almonds)

Directions

In a large skillet over medium-high heat, melt 1 teaspoon of Light butter or olive oil.

Add chicken and sauté for 3 to 4 minutes per side.

Remove and allow to rest on platter dish

Add remaining Light butter or olive oil to skillet. Allow to gradually begin to sizzle, turn down heat and then add shallots, leeks or onions and sauté for 30 seconds.

When liquid has nearly evaporated, add wine and tomatoes and continue to cook, while reducing heat.

Finally, add in wine, sour cream, basil and salt and pepper..

Recipe contribution by Linda Szantai

****

Marilyn's Manicotti Filling for Crepes

Ingredients

2 pounds of reduced fat or n-fat ricotta cheese

1 package (8 oz.) Part skim or no fat mozzarella cheese, diced

1-tablespoon parsley

1/3 cup Parmesan cheese

2 eggs (or egg substitute)

1-teaspoon salt

1/4 teaspoon pepper

Directions

Spread1/4 cup of filling into each manicotti crepe. Roll up. Place prepared spaghetti sauce in bottom of large pan or individual serving dishes. Place manicotti crepes over sauce and cover with additional sauce.

Bake at 350 degrees for approximately 20 - 25 minutes.

Recipe contribution by Marilyn Conklin

**See Marilyn's Manicotti crepes*

Marilyn's Manicotti Crepes

Ingredients

3 eggs

3 yolks (or egg substitutes)

2 cup flour

2 cup of 1% milk

3 tablespoons melted Light butter

3 tablespoons extra virgin Olive oil

Directions

Beat all ingredients until smooth. Let stand 2 hour.

Heat an 8 inch skillet.

Next, pour 3 tablespoons batter into pan and spread evenly.

Cook until top is dry but bottom is not brown.

Turn over and cook lightly on other side.

Stack with wax paper between each crepe. Freeze well.

*Note: These crepes lend themselves well for dessert trays as well.

Recipe contribution by Marilyn Conklin

****

Meat Loaf

Ingredients

1 to 1-1/2 pounds of ground round steak (all fat trimmed before grinding)

3/4 pound of lean pork (trimmed and ground)

Lite Soy sauce

Salt & pepper to taste (Sea salt)

1 tablespoon of Worcestershire sauce

Italian bread crumbs (2 cup)

1 slice of broken bread crumbs (whole grain bread)

2 diced large onion

2 diced jalapeno pepper

1 slightly beaten egg or egg substitute

Directions

In a large Mixing bowl, combine steak and pork

One by one add remaining ingredients and knead with hands until mixture stays together

*Add two tablespoons of ketchup to top of loaf and spread (optional)

Add 1/4 to 2 cup of water to bottom of baking pan

Bake at 350 degrees uncovered for about 1 2 hours

Grandma Kirk's Meatloaf

Ingredients

3-Pounds of very lean ground beef

1-Green pepper diced

4-Stalks of celery diced

3 to 4 handfuls of crushed corn flakes

2-Small onions diced

2-Eggs or Egg substitute equivalent

2-Cloves of minced Garlic or 1 Tsp. of dried Garlic

Directions

Preheat oven to 350 degrees

In a large mixing bowl, combine beef, green pepper, celery, onions and garlic with hands as though kneading dough.

When meat and vegetables are evenly distributed, add crushed corn flakes and eggs or egg substitute and mix well.

Form mixture into a loaf shape and place in a large cast iron skillet And bake for approximately 1-1/2 hours, draining excess fat whenever necessary from skillet.

Recipe contribution by Peggy Thubet

****

Pesto Pasta!

Ingredients

1- Cup (about 8 to 10 ounces) of Paul Newman's Pasta sauce. Choose; Roasted garlic, or Spicy red.

1 Diced red pepper (sweet)

1 Small onion diced

1 Tablespoon of crushed garlic

1 Jalapeno pepper (or 2 of pepper to taste)

Two (2) Tablespoons of Olive oil

Salt & Pepper to taste (Sea salt)

Shiitake mushrooms (2 cup)

Carrot shavings (about 1/4 cup)

2 cup of frozen white corn

1 cup of greens, either broccoli, kale, green beans or asparagus

2 cup Cooking Sherry

1/4 cup of frozen Okra

Fresh grated Italian cheese

Dash of Worcestershire sauce

Directions

In a large Skillet add Olive oil, sauté= red pepper, onion, garlic and red pepper for 4 to 5 minutes on low flame.

Add mushrooms, greens, Okra and Worcestershire sauce and continue to cook for another 5 minutes.

Add pasta sauce, corn and cooking wine and cook for remaining 5 or 6 minutes

Finally add carrot shavings and top with grated Italian cheese just before serving

Salt & pepper to taste.

****

Cajun Shrimp Casserole

Ingredients

1 to 1-1/2 cups of precooked rice

** When selecting rice, it is best to first concentrate on nutritional content of each, including carbohydrate grams, sodium and etc.*

1 Medium size onion diced

1-1/2 tablespoons of virgin Olive oil

2 cloves of minced fresh garlic

2 teaspoon of Sea salt

1 2 pounds of fresh cooked, shelled medium size Shrimp

2 cup of chopped red or yellow pepper

3/4 of a diced jalapeno pepper *optional

1 stalk of fresh organic celery (if not organic, clean and scrape exterior well)

1 cup of precooked Chinese cabbage (bokchoy)

1 tablespoon of Lite Soy sauce.

**Optional: Cayenne red pepper, corn and/or tomatoes*

Directions

Add 1 Tablespoon of virgin Olive oil to large skillet and heat

Add diced garlic, diced onion and jalapeno pepper along with yellow or red pepper and cook for about 2 minutes

Add diced celery and blanched Chinese celery and continue to cook on low heat for an additional 2 minutes.

Add cooked, shelled Shrimp to skillet and Sea Salt and continue to cook on low heat.

Add Lite Soy sauce

Add water as needed, including additional (2nd tablespoon of virgin Olive) oil.

Rice can be waiting in a medium size Serving dish and can be blended into Shrimp skillet or can be reheated using microwave oven for 1 minute just before serving.

If rice is served in separate dish, it can become the bed for the vegetables and Shrimp.

Fresh Italian bread completes this casserole dish!

****

Roast Leg Of lamb

Ingredients

Leg of Lamb roast (4 to 5 pounds)

Thyme

Rosemary

Parsley

Sage

Olive oil (preferably Extra Virgin)

Sea salt and pepper to taste

3 Large onions halved

Directions

Rinse lamb under running water for a couple of seconds to remove all paper, cellophane & etc.

Place in a Roasting pan

1 Tablespoonful of Rosemary

1 Tablespoonful of Thyme

½ Tablespoonful of Parsley

1/4 to ½ Tablespoonful of Sage

1 Tablespoonful of Olive oil.

In a small Mixing bowl, add; Rosemary, Thyme, Parsley, Sage and Olive oil. Gently blend herbs and Olive oil, and allow to sit for a few minutes until thoroughly blended.

With a small basting brush, apply blended herb mixture to the entire surface of the Lamb roast.

Coat Lamb a second time with blended herbs, using as much of the mixture as possible that will stick to the roast, and not drop off into the roasting pan.

Add 1/4 cup of cold water to the bottom of the roasting pan.

Replace lid on top of the roasting pan, and place into a pre-heated oven.

Bake at 325 to 350 degrees in the pre-heated oven.

Timing; Allow 40 minutes cooking time for each pound of lamb, or about 2 ½ to 3 hours. When meat is thoroughly cooked, it will begin to fall off bone.

Add halved onions to each side of the roast, after about 1 ½ hours of cooking time.

Roast should be basted every 30 minutes, and water added when necessary only.

A Side dish of greens, along with oven cooked onions top off this tasty meal!

Note: Leg of Lamb is one of the cuts of Lamb noted for its low amount of Saturated fat, other than the Shank, and is an excellent source of Protein, Potassium, Zinc, several of the B+ Complex vitamins and Amino Acids!

****

VEGETABLES

Not So Quiet, Hush Puppies

Ingredients

1 Egg Lightly beaten

1-1/3 cups of Buttermilk

½ Tsp. Of Sea Salt

½ Tsp. Pepper

1 Teaspoon of Baking Soda

3/4 cup of unbleached white All purpose flour

1-1/2 Cups of Cornmeal

2 Jalapeno peppers seeded and diced

2-Tablespoons of fresh Parsley (or 1 Tablespoon of dried Parsley)

3 Scallions chopped

Note: Strained oil (after use) can be refrigerated and reused again for up to 3 weeks.

Directions

In a medium size Mixing bowl, combine egg and Buttermilk and set aside.

In another bowl, add flour, cornmeal, Baking Soda, salt and pepper, and gently toss in Scallions, Jalapenos and Parsley.

Add in wet ingredients until evenly distributed, but do not over mix. Allow mixture to stand at room temperature for about 30 minutes.

In a large Skillet, heat 1" of Olive oil over medium heat, or until hot, but not smoking.

Carefully drop batter into skillet by the spoonful taking precaution to not over crowd skillet.

Turning only once until golden brown, or about two minutes per side.

Drain on paper towels before Serving.

Traditionally served with Catfish, this recipe will serve Six. See *Catfish* recipe.

285 Calories per Serving, 9 Grams of fat, 8 Grams of protein, 37 Mg. of Cholesterol, 44 Grams of Carbohydrates, 565 Grams of Sodium, 3 Grams of Fiber

****

LENTIL STUFFED PEPPERS

Ingredients

Four to Six peppers (yellow, red and green)

1-1/2 cups of cooked lentils

**Note: It is a good idea to cook the lentils and brown rice a day ahead, in order to save time.*

1-1/4 Cups of cook brown rice

1 Large Onion diced

**Optional*; ½ Cup of Shiitake or Maitake mushrooms

1 jalapeno pepper diced

3 to 4 cans (depending upon size and depth of Baking dish) of Low-Sodium Tomato soup

Add equal amount of water to each can of Tomato soup

1 Clove of Garlic diced

Dulse' Sea Salt or granulated Kelp (from a Shaker container) about 1/4 Teaspoon

Directions

In a Sauté pan, combine onion, jalapeno, garlic and mushrooms, along with one tablespoon of Extra Virgin Olive oil.

Sauté' for about 3 minutes until onions begin to appear translucent.

In a large Mixing bowl, combine rice, lentils, Sea Salt and mix together with a large spoon.

Now to the lentil and rice mixture, add the slightly cooked and cooled sautéed onion, garlic and etc.

While that is left to rest, begin to take washed peppers and cut and remove tops.

Peppers should be blanched in a large pot of lightly boiling water for about 1-1/2 minutes, or until slightly soft.

Note: ***Do Not Allow peppers to overcook*** *as they will begin to fall apart and will not hold mixture.*

In a large Baking dish, empty in slightly warmed tomato soup (mixed with water), soup can be warmed in microwave.

Scoop prepared lentil and rice mixture until all peppers are full. Arrange in Oven dish with Tomato Soup mixture, but do not overfill , or mixture will spill over when placed in heated Oven.

Leave approximately 3 to 4 inches from top of oven dish.

*Optional; Tops of peppers can be replaced onto respective peppers, and secured with wooden toothpicks, or waxed toothpicks (plastic may not fare well in oven temperatures).

Place dish in a preheated 325 to 350 degree oven in center of middle rack and allow to cook for an additional 35 to 40 minutes, or until peppers begin to lightly brown on tops.

Approximately 5 minutes before dish is done, remove from oven and sprinkle peppers with some low-fat cheese. Return to oven for 5 minutes, before removing.

Allow to cool for about 10 minutes.

Serve with some crusty bread and Sour cream (optional).

Cheesy Cauliflower

Ingredients

1- Head of washed and diced Cauliflower

Several pieces of Tofu cheese

1/4 Diced onion

Low-Sodium Soy Sauce (1 Tsp.)

1 Stalk of Celery

One Small diced tomato

½ Cup of diced Egg plant

4 Tofu dogs

1 Tablespoon of Olive oil

Directions

Sauté onion, celery, and cauliflower in Olive oil for about 7 minutes, tossing continuously.

Add Lite Soy Sauce, eggplant, tomatoes, tofu dogs, and continue to cook on low to medium heat.

Add diced tomato and water as needed and continue to cook for approximately another 5 minutes

Top with Tofu cheese and Serve!

****

Sweet potato fries

Ingredients

3 to 4 large sweet potatoes

Extra virgin olive oil

Nutmeg

Sea salt

Back pepper (or white)

Paprika

Directions

Clean potato skins & microwave for about 5 minutes

Allow to cool for 5 to 10 minutes

Cut potatoes lengthwise in 1 to 1 1/4 inch strips

Place on a cookie sheet

In a small mixing bowl combine 1 2 tablespoons of Olive oil, 1/4 tsp of nutmeg, and 1/4 tsp. of cloves (optional) stir together.

Place into a preheated oven of about 350 degrees for approximately 15 to 20 minutes, checking every 5 minutes as oven temperatures may vary.

When lightly browned, remove and sprinkle with salt and pepper to taste (including paprika).

****

Citrus Sweet Potatoes

Ingredients

2 to 3 pounds of Sweet potatoes (or about 8 yams or sweet potatoes)

2 whole oranges

3- tablespoons of light butter

2 tablespoons of water

2 to 3/4 cup of brown sugar or Date sugar

2 teaspoon of Sea salt

1/4 teaspoon of Nutmeg

1/4 teaspoon of Allspice

3 Tablespoons of chopped pecans or walnuts

Directions

~ Cook Sweet potatoes or yams in sufficient water for about 20 to 25 minutes, or until tender. for about 20 to 25 minutes, or until tender. Drain, peel and cut into ½ inch slices.

~ Grate orange peel (about 1 tablespoon) and set aside. Peel and slices oranges into thin slices.

~ In a baking dish, arrange alternate rows of sweet potato and orange slices.

~ In a small mixing bowl, combine Light butter, water, sugar, nutmeg and allspice.

~ Transfer to a small saucepan and slowly bring mixture to a boil while gradually adding in orange peel (finely grated.) As soon as mixture comes to a full boil, quickly remove from heat.

~ Drizzle mixture over sweet potatoes and orange slices which are already in a baking dish.

~ In a 325 degree heated oven, bake sweet potatoes and oranges for about 2 hour, or until mixture begins to glaze. For a consistent taste, spoon wet ingredients over mixture at least once while baking.

~ Before serving, once again baste sweet potatoes and orange slices with syrup at bottom of baking dish

~ Before serving, sprinkle chopped pecans or walnuts over sweet potatoes and

Orange slices. Serves 10

****

German Vegetable Mash

Ingredients

3-pounds of russet potatoes

3 carrots (scraped and cleaned) cut into slivered lengths

1-large Golden delicious apple peeled and diced into large slices

2-tablespoons of Light butter

1-tablespoon of grated Orange rind

¼ teaspoon of Allspice

½ cup of low fat milk

Directions

In a large stove top-cooking pan; add peeled potatoes, carrots, and Sliced Apple. Cover with water and cook over medium heat for 20 to 25 minutes, or until tender. When a fork placed into potatoes easily enters and exits without resistance, vegetables are done.

Drain potatoes and carrots (and apple) and transfer into a mixing bowl.

Add butter, Allspice and milk and beat on low speed for one minute. Add more liquid if necessary, continuing to beat on medium speed for one more minute.

Garnish with grated Orange rind and sprinkle over vegetable whip and Serve.

Note: Combining a variety of favorite vegetables with potatoes, such as; Garlic and Spinach, or Onion and Sweet peppers, quickly surpass the diner's usual expectations about

GRAVIES, SAUCES AND SOUPS

Barbecue Plum Sauce

Ingredients

1- Teaspoon of crushed red pepper

1- Teaspoon dried gingerroot

2- Garlic cloves minced

1- Tablespoon of Light Teriyaki sauce

1 Teaspoon of dried mustard powder, or 1 Tablespoon of prepared mustard

1/3 cup of Chili sauce

1- Large onion chopped

1-20 Ounce can whole unpitted purple plums

1-Small (6ounce) can of thawed lemonade frozen concentrate

Directions

Strain plums reserving syrup. Pit plums.

In a blender, combine onion, lemonade concentrate, chili sauce, mustard and pitted plums, Teriyaki sauce, garlic, gingerroot, and crushed red pepper. Place lid on top of blender and blend until smooth.

Empty blender contents into medium size saucepan and heat over medium heat until boiling, reduce heat and continue to simmer for about 45 minutes, stirring frequently. Allow to cool, and place in a clean glass jar with lid and refrigerate until the next barbecue.

About 30 minutes before placing onto heated Barbecue, pour sufficient amount of barbecue Plum sauce into bowl large enough to hold pork chops, or ribs. Marinate for 30 minutes before placing on barbecue.

****

Chicken Soup In A Jiffy

Ingredients

2-Cubes of Low-Sodium bullion

2-Quarts of water

2-Stalks of fresh celery cleaned and diced

2-Tablespoons of Virgin Olive oil

1-Medium sized onion diced

*1-Small jalapeno pepper (optional) seeded and diced.

1-Large carrot cleaned and sliced in 2 inch sections

½ Teaspoon of dried parsley

1-Medium sized ripe tomato sliced

½ cup of Okra (frozen)

2-Potatoes peeled and diced

¼ cup of Cooking Sherry

2-Tablespoons of cut Garlic (fresh or prepared as prepared has no negative additives)

Directions

In a large cooking pot, add two quarts of water and the two Low-Sodium bullion cubes.

Cook cubes on medium heat.

Meanwhile, in a large skillet, and on a low flame, add Olive oil, and add Garlic, onion, cut celery and jalapeno pepper and cook over medium for 2 to 3 minutes, or until onions begin to become transparent, but not browned.

Add cut carrots, dried parsley and sliced tomato and continue to cook.

Note: When the liquid at bottom of skillet begins to evaporate, add cooking Sherry.

Add Okra and diced potatoes to water with bullion cubes and continue to cook on low to medium heat.

When skillet vegetables have reached a deeper color and are just beginning to brown.

Remove from flame and add to water and bullion mixture and stir.

Continue to cook for another 10 to 12 minutes on medium heat until potatoes are tender.

Remove from heat, cover and allow to rest.

Serve with a crusted bread.

****

SAUCES

Blueberry Sauce

Ingredients

1-cup of fresh or frozen blueberries

¾ cup of burgundy wine

¼ cup of raw sugar

1/6 teaspoon of crushed rosemary

¼ cup of water

1-tablespoon cornstarch

2- tablespoons cold Light butter

2-tablespoons heavy cream

Directions

Combine blueberries, water, sugar, rosemary and wine in a small saucepan and slowly bring to a boil, reduce heat and continue to simmer for an additional 5 minutes.

Mix cream and cornstarch together in a small mixing bowl until thoroughly combined.

Puree and strain blueberry mixture, return to a simmer on low heat.

Turn heat down to Low and incorporate butter into sauce while continuing to stir.

Once butter has melted, remove sauce from heat and discontinue simmering!

****

Holiday Cherry Sauce

This sauce is great when serving turkey, stuffing and etc.

Ingredients

1 cup of low-sodium chicken bullion

1 cup of unsweetened cherry juice

1/4 cup of chopped onion

2 cup of dried cherries minced

1 teaspoon of minced dried Thyme

1 Tablespoon of white wine

1/4 tsp. White pepper

1/4 cup unsweetened cherry juice

1-teaspoon sugar

3 teaspoons of cornstarch

Directions

In a small pan, combine chicken bullion, 1 cup of unsweetened cherry juice, onion, dried cherries, white wine Thyme, white pepper and sugar. Over medium heat, stirring occasionally, bring to a full boil. Reduce heat and allow to simmer to an additional 10 to 12 minutes.

Meanwhile, combine 1/4 cup of cherry juice and cornstarch.

Transfer to pan which has been simmering. Continue to cook (about 1-1/2 to 2 min.) Until mixture begins to bubble and has taken on a thicker consistency. Serve warm with turkey, makes about two cups.

****

Honey Mustard

Ingredients

1/4 cup of dry mustard

1-1/2 Tablespoons of cornstarch

2 Teaspoon of crushed dried tarragon

1/4 Teaspoon of Sea salt

2 Teaspoon of Tumeric

1/4 cup of honey

1 Tablespoon of virgin Olive oil

1 Cup of water

1-1/2 Tablespoons of dry white wine

Directions

In a small cooking utensil, add mustard, cornstarch, water, tarragon, Tumeric and Sea salt.

Stir while cooking on low to medium heat, stirring constantly until mixture becomes smooth, bubbly and has noticeably thickened.

Continue to cook for about another two to three minutes, stirring continuously.

Add in honey, oil and white wine.

Cover top of pot with plastic wrap and allow to rest for about ten minutes.

When mixture has sufficiently cooled, pour into glass jar,
or several small jars with secure lids and store in refrigerator.

Makes two 3/4 cup portions, and makes a nice contribution to any Covered dish dinner.

****

Lickety-Split Pea Soup

Ingredients

2-Quarts of water

2-Low-Sodium bullion cubes

1-Diced carrot

1-chopped onion (medium sized)

½-Teaspoon of dried Dill weed

1-Cup of diced Canadian bacon

1-Cup of fully cooked skinned, boned chicken breast

1-Pound of split peas, cleaned and drained

2-Stalks of chopped celery

1-Medium size ripe tomato

½-Teaspoon of white pepper

2-Large peeled, diced potatoes

Directions

In a large pot, add water and bullion cubes and heat on medium heat Add peas and allow water to come to a full boil, quickly turning down heat and continuing to cook for twenty t twenty-five minutes over medium flame.

After the peas have been cooking for approximately 25 minutes, add Other ingredients, saving chicken and Canadian bacon however, for the last fiver minutes of cooking.

Note: The precooked chicken and/or ham need only to be heated, And not re-cooked.

*Optional~ Sprinkle top of soup with ***Veggie Topping by Galaxy Foods.***

It is made with Organic tofu, Garlic and Herb flavor. It is no fat, low-Sodium, no sugar, and is only 15 Calories for 2 teaspoons contains 2 grams of protein. It can be a good substitute for other higher fat toppings such as grated cheese.

Galaxy Foods are manufactured in Orlando, Florida.

****

Roasted Garlic Sauce

Ingredients

2/3-Quart of "Half-n-Half" or Light cream (For less Fat & Calories, use Carnation Skimmed canned milk, or combine ½ Carnation Skim milk to ½ of Lite "Half-n-Half).

1-Fresh whole garlic unpeeled (a Baker's dozen)

Sea salt and white pepper to taste

Directions

Place garlic in a clay oven cooker, or on a cookie sheet and bake in a 400-degree oven for 20 to 25 minutes, or until light brown and soft to touch.

Remove outer peel of garlic and place in a small saucepan. Add cream to garlic pan and simmer on low-to-medium heat until mixture is reduced to about ½ quart. Add Sea salt and white pepper

****

DESSERTS AND BAKED GOODS

Hawaiian delight

Ingredients

1-Package of miniature marshmallows

1-Package of Shredded Coconut

1-Can of Crushed pineapple

1-16 Ounce package of Sour Cream

2-Small cans of Mandarin oranges

Directions

In a large mixing bowl, combine all ingredients and allow to rest over night in the refrigerator.

Serve on a bed of lettuce.

*A small can of decorative cherries can be added last. Do not add until ready to serve as cherries may discolor other ingredients.

Recipe contribution by Margie Dewar

****

Healthier Cheesecake

Ingredients

2 cups of Golden Grahams cereal

1/4 cup of olive oil

2- 12 oz. Packages of fat-free cream cheese

1 2 cartons of Egg Substitute (equal to 3-eggs)

2 cup of date sugar

1/4 to 2 cup of frozen white grape juice concentrate (made from pure concentrate and **not** containing high fructose syrup.

1 tablespoon of lemon extract

1 tablespoon of vanilla

1 package of Lite tofu

2 tablespoons of flour

Directions

Chop cereal in a blender until texture is fine.

In a medium sized bowl, and cereal crumbs, date sugar and white grape frozen concentrate and blend together

Take this mixture and press into the bottom of a 9" round cake pan sprayed with non-stick vegetable oil.

Bake at 325 degrees for about 5 or 6 minutes.

Allow to sit and cool while you take remaining ingredients and place in a blender

Mix at low speed for a couple of minutes until smooth consistency.

Pour mixture over baked crust and bake at 450 degrees for about 10 minutes.

Reduce heat after 10 minutes to 250 degrees and continue to bake for about 50 minutes. Cool.

Top with a "Light" pie filling of your choice over cake and chill till ready to serve.

**This dessert is about 100 Calories per serving with 0 grams of fat.*

****

Healthier “No-Bake” Cheesecake

Ingredients

Fat free cream cheese (16 oz. Package)

3/4 cup of unprocessed sugar

1/4 cup of plain fat free yogurt

1/4 cup of fat free sour cream

2 cup of low fat whipped topping

1 teaspoon of vanilla

2 teaspoon unflavored gelatin mixed together with 1 tablespoon of water

2 cup of white chocolate chips, melted Graham cracker crust

Graham cracker crust

2/3 cup of unbleached all purpose flour

1-1/4 cup of whole-wheat flour

* *Individuals with a gluten intolerance may substitute wheat flour for Soy, Millet or any other whole grain organic flour.*

1 Teaspoon of Sea salt

3 Tablespoons of dark brown sugar (or Date sugar)

1 2 Tablespoons of Black Strap molasses

1 Tablespoon of pure Vanilla extract

1 Tablespoon of water

2 Tablespoons of "Light" butter

Nutritional analysis; *Each serving contains about 110 calories, 5 grams of fat, 2 grams of protein and 16 grams of carbohydrate.*

Less than 1 gram of saturated fat.

Directions

Preheat oven to 325 degrees.

Spray a Cookie sheet with nonstick vegetable spray

Roll out the above dough mixture on cookie sheet in a thin, evenly distributed mixture without breaking apart.

Place in oven and bake for about 15 minutes or until lightly browned

Allow dough mixture (looks like a large cookie) to cool

Place dough mixture after it has cooled into blender in large pieces and finely blend. ~ Add melted butter.

Add water

Gently mix together

Press moistened mixture (crumbs by now) on the bottom and sides of a greased Spring form pan

Add cheesecake filling and bake as directed in individual recipe.

Directions for "No-Bake" Cheesecake Filling

**Cheesecake crust can be made the day before in order to save time*

After preparing crust mixture as instructed, blend together cheesecake and sugar with electric Mixer.

Next; Combine yogurt, topping, Sour Cream, white chocolate Lemon juice and Vanilla Extract.

Blend until mixture is smooth and evenly distributed throughout mixture.

Drizzle gelatin mixture over and fold in gently.

Pour batter into prepared crust and pat gently with a small spatula until smooth

Cover with a plastic wrap and refrigerate for 2 to 2-1/2 hours, or until set

Serves 8. Nutritional analysis; Calories 210, per serving, 5 grams of protein, 3 grams of fat, 100 milligrams of sodium and 20 grams of carbohydrate.

****

Chocolate Oatmeal Cookies

Ingredients

Dry

2 cup of packed brown sugar

2 cup of Date sugar

1 Teaspoon of Baking Soda

1 Tablespoon of Cinnamon

1 cup Unbleached organic white flour

1 2 cup of rolled oats

2 cup of Soy flour

1 cup of Millet flour

1 cup of Carob, or Chocolate chips

Wet

4-Ounce jar of strained Baby food, Applesauce, or Peaches.

Two tablespoons of Black-Strap Molasses

8-Oz. Brown Rice Syrup

1 Tablespoon of Vanilla Extract

Two egg whites

1/3 cup of Olive oil

Instructions

In a large bowl mix dry ingredients together, and in another bowl lightly beat wet ingredients.

Slowly add dry ingredients to wet ingredients, with the last ingredient being the chocolate chips.

Drop by teaspoon onto lightly greased cookie trays.

Place in preheated 350-degree oven for 14 to 17 minutes.

Makes three to three, and a half dozen cookies.

****

Chocolate Muffins

Ingredients

1 and 3/4 cups of Unbleached white pastry flour

1 tablespoon of Baking powder

1/4 teaspoon of Baking soda

Dash of Salt

1/3 cup of Virgin Olive oil

1 egg (beaten)

1 cup of Plain yogurt

1/3 cup of Date sugar, or Light brown sugar

2 cup of Soy (or Rice) Milk

!/2 cup of Chopped Walnuts (optional)

1/3 Cup of Dry Cocoa mix

1 Teaspoon of Instant Coffee (optional)

Confectioners Sugar

Directions

Either spray muffin tray with an oil, or use paper inserts

Combine all dry ingredients together

Add lightly beaten egg oil, and other wet ingredients.

Beat for about 40 Strokes by hand, then spoon into Muffin tray, remembering not to fill cups more than 2/3 full.

Place in a 325 degree preheated oven for 25 to 30 minutes.

Allow to cool, then sprinkle lightly with confectioners sugar.

Store in an airtight plastic container in the refrigerator for up to one week, or freeze.

Frozen muffins can be thawed in the microwave oven on low setting for 45 seconds to one minute.

To warm from the refrigerator, place in the microwave oven on "Warm Setting" for 20 to 30 seconds.

****

Chocolate Peanut Butter Cookies

Ingredients

2 cup of Date sugar

2 3/4 Tablespoons of peanut butter

1 Tablespoon of Olive oil

1 Egg or equivalent egg substitute

1 Tablespoon of pure Vanilla extract

1 large ripe banana mashed

2 cup of low fat plain yogurt

1 teaspoon of baking powder

3/4 teaspoon of baking soda

3/4 cup of unbleached organic white flour

3 or 4 Tablespoons of Semi-sweet chocolate chips or carob chips

Preheat oven to 375 degrees

Directions

Spray 12 Muffin cups with a nonstick vegetable spray

In a large mixing bowl, combine sugar, oil, peanut butter, egg, banana, yogurt, vanilla extract and mix.

In a separate bowl, combine flour, baking soda, baking powder and blend. Add chocolate chips and blend.

Add dry ingredients to wet and blend.

Fill muffin cups to half way mark. Bake in preheated oven of 375 degrees for 15 to 18 minutes.

Tops should be firm to touch, and cake tester should come out dry when inserted into muffins.

Note: Each Serving contains approximately 125 Calories, 20 grams of Carbohydrates, 8 grams of fiber, 4 grams of fat, and 105 mg. of Sodium.

****

Cranberry-Nut Bread

Ingredients

1-1/2 cups of all purpose unbleached organic flour

2 tsp. Of baking soda

1 teaspoon of baking powder

Note; This is where one can begin to experiment with flours by using combinations, such as; 1 cup unbleached white flour and one cup of Soy, Millet, Kamut, Corn or another whole grain of choice; Rice, Barley and etc. Visit your local Health Food Store and examine what is available!

3/4 cup of brown sugar, date sugar, or perhaps 1 jar of strained pureed baby food such as prunes, or peaches.

2 cup of Orange juice

1/3 to 2 cup of Virgin Olive oil.

1 teaspoon of ground cinnamon

1 teaspoon of ground cloves

1 cup of either dried pitted cherries or dried cranberries

1/4 cup of dried blueberries, or raisins

1/4 cup of chopped pecans.

* Raisins are best purchased in organic form as processed raisins contain more pesticide residues than many other processed foods, nearly 100.

Directions

In a large mixing bowl, combine flour, baking powder, baking soda, Baking powder and cloves. Stir together, gradually including cloves. In another medium size mixing bowl, mix eggs, brown sugar (or Date sugar),

Orange juice and Olive oil. After thoroughly and gently mixing, add to flour mixture, continuing to stir. Now add in cranberries, cherries, (or Dates), blueberries (or raisins), and pecans.

Whether using large baking pan, or several smaller ones, add batter to about halfway mark.

At 300 degrees, bake batter for 45 to 50 minutes, or until toothpick test shows bread is done (when toothpick comes out clean, after insertion into dough).

Cool loaves on center rack for 10 minutes.

*Optional; Loaves can be wrapped in cheesecloth which has been soaked in Cheesecloth. Cover Cheesecloth with Aluminum foil and store in refrigerator. Will be edible for up to 2 months.

****

Holiday Bread

Ingredients

1 package of dry yeast

2 cup of luke warm water

2 to 3 tablespoons of sugar

1- 12 ounce can of evaporated skim milk

2 teaspoon of Sea salt

4 cups of all purpose unbleached organic white flour

**organic is optional*

2 tablespoons of virgin olive oil

1/4 teaspoon of ground ginger

1 - egg

Directions

Empty the package of dry yeast along with ½ cup of warm water into a small pot and keep warm at a temperature of approximately 120 degrees.

In a large mixing bowl, combine 1 2 cups of flour, and ginger.

Add yeast mixture to flour mixture, and add milk, stirring by hand .

Add as much remaining flour as possible without becoming too dry.

Place dough mixture onto a lightly floured surface.

Knead in a sufficient amount of flour to make a stiff dough consistency, yet remain smooth and elastic.

Form dough into a ball, and place into a glass greased bowl and cover. Turn once after a couple of minutes in order to grease both sides.

Allow dough to rest at room temperature for about 45 minutes and rise.

After 45 minutes has elapsed, take dough and punch down, turn onto a lightly floured surface and divide in two.

Once again; cover and allow to rest for an additional 10 minutes.

Moderately grease a large baking sheet and sprinkle with cornmeal.

Form each half of dough into a ball, and place on baking sheet.

Two halves can also be transferred into two individual greased 8 X 4 X 2" loaf pans.

Break egg and add 1 tablespoon of water.

Brush onto top of loaves. With a sharp knife, cut an X onto the tops of each loaf.

Cover and allow to rise once again in a warm place until they have almost doubled in size, usually this will take about 30 minutes.

Bake in a preheated 350-degree oven for 35 to 40 minutes, or until bread tests have been done (you may take a tooth pick and insert it into each loaf, and if it comes out dry, bread is done).

To prevent over-baking the tops of the loaves, place aluminum foil loosely over tops of each loaf for the final 15 minutes of baking time.

Allow to cool on racks for fifteen minutes and half hour before cutting.

****

PINEAPPLE-APPLE KUGEL

Ingredients

½ Pound of Small to Medium Egg noodles

½ cup or 1 Stick of butter (Convert to ¼ cup of Virgin Olive oil + ¼ cup of Light butter to ensure a healthier recipe.)

3 Eggs lightly beaten (or equivalent egg beaters)

3-Tablespoons of Sugar (convert to strained baby foods or unsweetened frozen white grape juice concentrate (undiluted) for a healthier recipe)

1-Teaspoon of ground cinnamon

1-Tablespoon of pure vanilla

½ cup of raisins (Organic raisins are recommended to avoid pesticide residues from processing)

1-Cup of Sour cream (Convert to Low-Fat or No-Fat for healthier recipe)

1-8 Ounce can of Crushed pineapples drained

3-Tablespoons of Vegetable oil (convert to Virgin or Extra Virgin Olive oil for a healthier recipe)

1-Large Apple peeled and chopped

¼ to ½ Cup of Walnut or Pecan pieces (avoid peanuts whenever possible)

Directions

Preheat oven to 350 degrees F.

Lightly grease (using baking spray or Virgin Olive oil) a 9" Baking loaf pan

Place cooked noodles in a pot, adding butter and/or oil, allowing sufficient time for butter to melt in hot noodles.

In a small Mixing bowl, lightly beat eggs; Add in vanilla and cinnamon. Fold egg mixture into noodles

Add in remaining ingredients to noodles; Pineapple, apple, raisins and sour cream, stirring until thoroughly blended.

Transfer mixture into lightly greased baking loaf pan and sprinkle tope with nuts.

Bake at 350 degree preheated oven for 50 to 60 minutes.

****

Millet Bread

Ingredients

Profile; Each slice of Millet bread contains; 100 Calories, 0.5 grams of Saturated fat, 0-Cholesterol, 170 Milligrams of Sodium, 130 grams of Potassium, 2 Slices equals 260 milligrams of Potassium, and while bananas contain 390 Milligrams of potassium, they also contain 21 grams of carbohydrate, and only 1 gram of fiber, and 3 grams of sugar

Note; See other bread recipes, and incorporate Millet into recipe by simply using ½ of flour called for rather than total amount, and ½ of Millet flour.

Many of these breads can be found in the Freezer section of your local Health-Food Stores.

****

Millet Pudding

Millet is a highly nutritious grain and contains a multitude of both Vitamins and Minerals, including a high amount of natural Calcium, and ounce for ounce more Potassium than a Banana.

Ingredients

1-1/2 cups of dry Millet grain (fluffy and separates much like rice)

3 2 cups of water to each 1-1/2 cups of Millet grain

1-Tsp. Cinnamon

1 Tablespoon of pure Vanilla extract

Directions

In a medium size pot add water and Millet

Cook on medium heat for a couple of minutes

Add Vanilla and Cinnamon

Simmer on low to medium heat for approximately 45 minutes to an hour.

Check pot frequently, adding low fat milk or water as necessary to prevent sticking, stirring as needed.

When cooking is complete (grain will be soft), allow to cool for 15 minutes. Transfer to individual serving dishes

Top with a No fat topping. Refrigerate until ready to Serve.

Note: For individuals with allergic reaction to gluten, Millet contains no gluten.

Millet is a bland and mild grain and combines well with apples, surpasses Wheat and/or Brown rice in many B+ vitamins and in several essential Minerals such as Copper, Iron & etc.

OAT BREAD

Ingredients

¾ to 1 cup of rolled oats

4 ½ to 5 cups of All-purpose unbleached flour

¾ cup of 1% milk

2 packages of dry yeast

2 to 3 tablespoons of Brown sugar

¼ cup of Virgin Olive oil

2 eggs or egg substitute

1/3 cup of Oats rolled in Black Strap Molasses

1-1/2 cups of Oat bran

Directions

In a medium saucepan, bring 1-1/2 cups of water to boiling point; add the ¾ cup of rolled oats and reduce heat to a simmer for about 7 to 8 minutes.

Water will be nearly completely absorbed when oats are done. Remove from heat and let stand for 10 minutes. Oats should be medium warm for next procedure.

In a large Mixing bowl, flour (1-1/2 cups), and yeast, set aside.

In a small cooking pot, heat milk, sugar, butter and Seal salt until just warm (about 120 degrees), butter should be nearly melted. Add to flour mixture and blend.

Add to flour; Eggs and beat on low speed for about 30 seconds, scraping sides of bowl often. Beat on high speed for about 2 minutes. With a wooden spoon stir in cooled oat mixture, oat bran and black strap molasses. Use as much of flour as possible, without drying out mixture too much.

Lightly flour your counter top work are, and turn dough out. Knead in remaining flour while continuing to knead. Dough should be moderately stiff, yet smooth and elastic.

This usually requires about 8 minutes of kneading. It is important however, not to over-knead as dough will be harder to work with.

Put dough in a lightly greased bowl and allow to rest , turning once to saturate both sides of dough with Olive oil.

Cover and let rise in a warm place until dough has doubled in size, or about an hour.

Return dough mixture to lightly floured counter surface area and punch dough down, turning from side to side.

Divide dough into two equal halves. Shape dough into nine equal sized balls and place into two (2) greased pans. Either two 8 X 1-1/2 inch round baking pans, or two (2) 8 x 8 x 2 inch pans will do. Cover each pan and allow to rise until dough almost doubles. Rising should take approximately 40 minutes.

Dip a cooking brush into warm milk and brush the tops of the nine balls, and sprinkle with oats.

Turn oven to 375 degrees and bake bread for 30 to 35 minutes or until bread sounds hollow when tapped with a utensil. If necessary, and because oven temperatures may vary, bread can be cooked an additional 10 minutes, or until tops are lightly browned, but not over-cooked.

Peanut Butter Cookies

Ingredients

Dry	Wet
1 Cup of Date Sugar	2 cup of Olive oil
1 Tsp. Baking Soda	1 whole egg
2 Tsp. Baking Powder (non-Aluminum type) ~	1 Tsp. Pure Vanilla Extract
Dash of Salt	2 cup of Vanilla Soy milk
1 2 cups of Unbleached organic white flour	2 Tablespoons of Soy-Nut Butter
1 cup of organic Soy flour	Blackberry- "All-Fruit" Jelly, or any other of your favorite All fruit Jelly flavors.

*Optional – One cup of chopped Walnuts

Directions

In a large Mixing bowl, combine Sugar, Egg, and oil.

Blend for 30 seconds on Low Speed with hand Mixer.

Add baking powder, baking soda, salt, and vanilla.

Next; Slowly add flour and milk, alternating one, and the other until evenly mixed.

Drop onto lightly greased Cookie sheet with a Teaspoon.

Bake at 350 degrees in a pre-heated oven for 14 to 16 minutes.

Variation suggestion: When cookies have baked for about ten minutes, bring out, and add 1/4 Tsp. Of Jelly to the tops, lightly depressing each cookie. Or, prior to placing into a pre-heated oven, place one Walnut in the center of each cookie.

When fully cooled, place in a sealed container and refrigerate.

They should remain fresh for one week, without freezing.

Note: Because these "Cookie Cakes" are very moist, they must be adequately cooked, and to do so without burning bottoms, a double insulated Cookie Sheet is recommended.

****

Pound Cake

Ingredients

Dry	Wet
3-Cups of Cake flour	½ cup "Lite" butter
1/2 Tsp. Salt	½ cup of Brown Rice Syrup
3-Teaspoons of "Aluminum-free" Baking powder	3 Egg-whites-and-1-whole Egg
2 cup of Date Sugar	1-Cupof No-fat Sour Cream
	Teaspoon of Vanilla Extract

***Optional** ~ 1 cup of Dry Walnuts, or Pecans

Note: ½ Cup of Cocoa powder can be substituted for 2 cup of Cake flour.

Directions

In a large bowl, mix dry ingredients together. In a separate bowl, lightly blend wet ingredients, then slowly incorporate dry ingredients into wet ingredients. Lightly spray an 8 2 or 9" Loaf pan, and bake in a preheated 350 degree oven for 1 hour.

****

Pumpkin Bread

Ingredients

3 cups of Sugar (healthier substitute would be 1 cup of Date Sugar plus 2 jars of Strained Baby food such as unsweetened Applesauce or bananas)

4 beaten eggs (healthier choices might be 2 eggs, plus 2 egg whites, or egg-substitute equivalent to 4 eggs.)

Sixteen ounce can of pumpkin or equivalent fresh pumpkin cooked and strained

¼ to 1/3 cup of water

3 ½ cups of Unbleached all purpose flour (With experimentation for taste, an incorporation of other flours might be substituted for 1 cup of white unbleached flour)

8 Ounce package of pitted Dates

One cup of Virgin Olive oil

½ teaspoon of pure Vanilla

One teaspoon of Baking soda

A teaspoon of Sea Salt

Cup (1) of either chopped Walnuts, or Pecans

Directions

In a large Mixing bowl, combine sugar, eggs, pumpkin, oil vanilla and water until thoroughly blended.

In another bowl, combine flour, Baking soda, cinnamon and Sea salt

Incorporate flour into pumpkin, or wet ingredients continuing to gently stir. When mixture is smooth and completely distributed, add in dates and nuts.

Preheat oven to 350 degrees

Lightly grease two 9 x 5 x 3-inch baking pans

Bake in oven for 50 to 60 minutes, use toothpick test to see if center of loaves are done

Cool for 15 minutes before serving, or wrapping to store in refrigerator

****

Pumpkin Cookies

Ingredients

Dry	Wet
Two cups of unbleached Pastry flour	2 cup of Olive oil
2 Tsp. Of Cinnamon	1-Banana mashed
2 Tsp. Powdered Ginger.	1- large egg
1/4 Tsp. Nutmeg	½ cup of Pumpkin puree
1 cup of Date sugar (or brown sugar)	
1/4 Tsp. Of Sea Salt	
1 Teaspoon of Baking Soda	

Directions

In a large Mixing bowl, add dry ingredients and combine. Add wet ingredients and blend lightly.

Drop by Teaspoon onto lightly sprayed insulated Cookie sheet, and bake in a 350-degree pre-heated oven for 14 to 16 minutes.

* **Optional~** After cookies have completely cooled on a wire rack for one hour, dip one half of cookie in Steels Fudge sauce, and refrigerate. Cookies will remain fresh for one week in refrigerator.

Note: For Diabetics it is recommended that Date sugar be used, rather than Brown sugar. And oil can be replaced with Fruit puree. See Resource chapter for ordering products.

CHAPTER FIVE

Resources

This Chapter will provide resources for locating many of the healthier food replacements suggested throughout this Holistic CookBook.

Organic Growers And Suppliers

FOOD FOR LIFE BAKING CO., INC.
2991 EAST DOHERTY STREET,
CORONA, CA. 91719
1-800-797-5090

GREAT AMERICAN NATURAL PRODUCTS, INC.
4121--16TH STREET NORTH,
ST. PETERSBURG, FLORIDA 33703
1-800-323-4372

HEALTH VALLEY FOODS
700 UNION STREET,
MONTEBELLO, CA. 90640
(213)-724-2211

NESHAMINY VALLEY FOODS
NATURAL FOODS DISTRIBUTOR LIMITED,
5 LOUISE DRIVE,
IVYLAND, PA. 18974 (215) 443-5545

FAX# 9215) 443-7087

NOTE: Any or all of the above resources may have moved, changed their phone numbers, or ceased to do business. They are offered only because they have been at this writing, or in the past.

.

Reference Books, And Other Potential For More Health Food Growers/Resources A CONSUMER'S DICTIONARY OF MEDICINES, PRESCRIPTIONS, AND OVER-THE-COUNTER (PLUS HERBAL) ~With Medical Definitions

By; Ruth Winter, M.S.

Published by Crown Trade Paperbacks 1993 (A revised copy may be available.)

.

DIET FOR A POISONED PLANET

By David Steinman Published by Harmony Books 1990

HEINERMAN'S ENCYCLOPEDIA OF FRUITS, VEGETABLES AND HERBS

By: John Heinerman Published by Parker Publishing

NUTRITION ALMANAC

By Lavon J. Dunne Published by McGraw Hill Publishing (3rd edition)

Sold 2.5 million copies

500 FAT FREE RECIPES

BY Sarah Schlesinger

Published by Villard Books, Div. Of Random House 1994

****

RESOURCES

Additives~ An International Association offering information and support on food additives related to health problems is the Feingold Association P.O. Box 6550, Alexandria, VA. 2206,
Telephone (703) 768-3287. They also publish a Newsletter "Pure Facts" ten times a year.

Flour (unbleached and organic)~ Hodgson Mill is often available in many Super Markets, and offers Unbleached white flour, and "Whole grain and Stone ground whole wheat flours." To purchase many of the organic flours mentioned earlier on in the first couple of chapters in this book, such as Spelt, Kamut, Soy, Rice, Buckwheat and others, Arrowhead Mills is one of a number of the few Manufacturers who supply these flours. Usually, they are only found in Health Food Stores at this time, and that is probably due to their short span "Shelf-Life" as they must be refrigerated because they are "live" with nutrients that are spoilable. Arrowhead Mills is located at Box 2059, Hereford, Texas 79045, and offers no toll free number.

Date Sugar~ Tree of Life, St. Augustine, Florida 32085, Toll free number 1-800-874-0851. Other products include; Unsulphured Dried Fruit, Whole grains, Flour, Beans, Nuts, Seeds, Pasta, Cookies, Fruit Bars, natural fruit juices, Cheeses, Peanut Butter, oils and Tofu.

Meat and Poultry (Organic)~ Chicken and beef hot dogs, whole chickens, and beef , including bologna and ground meat made without using harmful Nitrites, or Nitrates, devoid of food colorings. And only organic grains are feed to the animals.

Garden Spot Distributors; 438 White Oak Road, Box 729A, New Holland, PA. 17557. Call (800)-829-5100.

Another is; **Brae Beef** 45 John Street, Greenwich, CT. 06831 at (203) 869-0106.

And for a third source; **Green Earth Natural Foods,** 2545 Prairie Avenue, Evanston, IL. 60201, call (800) 322-3662.

Pie filling, Pancake Syrup and Sugar-free Chocolate Syrup~ Using Sweeteners such as "Maltitol" (derived from corn, it is converted first to "Maltisorb" and Crystalline Fructose (also derived from a Corn source), and neither of which leave an after-taste.

Steel's Gourmet Foods, Continental Business Center, Suite D-175, Bridgeport, PA. 19405. They carry twenty seven products, including everything from Pie Fillings, to Maple Syrup and Fudge Sauce, to Jams, and can be reached Toll free at 1-800-6-Steels or Fax (610)-277-1228.

Portable Water filters~ General Ecology ~ 151 ~ Sheree Boulevard, Lionville, PA. 19353, or call toll free at (800) 441-8166. They manufacture the "First Need" portable drinking water purifier.

Safe Home Products~ A State chartered institute that provides educational materials about home and water hazards associated with industrial pollution and natural causes. They can be contacted at Environmental Hazards Management Institute Box 932, Durham, NH 03824, or call (603) 868-1496.

Soy nut Butter~(organic) Made from dry roasted Soybeans.

Other ingredients include;   Canola oil, Soy Lecithin, and Sea Salt. Made by Health Trip P.O. Box 507, Concord, MA. 01742. Call toll free 1-888-270-9688.

Lighter Bake~   This is a 100% FAT-free butter and oil replacement made from a fruit puree of dried Plums and Apples. "Lighter Bake" is a Trademark of Sunsweet Growers Inc., and is packed by Sunsweet Growers Inc. In Yuba City, California 95993-9370 U.S.A. They can be reached at 1-800-417-2253.

Moroccan Vegetarian Meal (organic)~   A frozen Entree= which consists of Bulgur wheat, Lentils, Garbanzo beans, vegetables, and raisins with exotic North African Seasonings. It is low in fat at four grams (with no saturated fat), and high in fiber.

Read ingredient labels, and select only those Entree dishes such as the Moroccan Vegetarian Meal, that has no food additives, or Preservatives, food colorings, or hydrogenated oils. A frozen Entree distributed by Cascadian Farm, Rockport, WA. 98283. You can also locate them On-Line at www.cfarm.com or at 719 Metcalf Street, Sedro-Woolley, WA. 98284 USA.

GLOSSARY

Denatured~~ *This is a term given to a substance which has been altered synthetically, or to describe a component, or substance which does not come to us In the same chemically organic manner in which Nature has provided.*

Devitalized~ *A food which has had its natural nutrients removed in order to prevent spoilage is considered to be a devitalized food. With the addition of specific food preservatives, the Manufacturers lengthen the amount of Shelf-life time. se Often minimal amounts of one, or two synthetic vitamins are then replaced into these devitalized foods, in order to gain the FDA's (Food And Drug Administration) approval.*

Glossary of Government Agencies

FDA~ The Food And Drug Administration is an Agency elected by the Federal Government to review products for potential "Approval" onto the Market, especially food. It is their responsibility to analyze all relative available literature for each food product, and to set limitations for various Food Additives and Food Preservatives. according to their proven safety, or potential risk for disease, and determine "Tolerable" levels for these additives. The FDA can be reached during regular Business hours (Eastern Standard Time) at 1-800-332-4010.

GRAS~ Generally Regarded As Safe is a term often used for various Additives which have been deemed as safe, and therefore enjoy the freedom of "No Limitations" regarding their use as presently used. However; many times over, similar products have been given the "Green Light", or the GRAS stamp of approval by the FDA, yet may one day be recalled. Regardless however, of the FDA'S ultimate decision regarding various "Additives, and or Preservatives", it is ultimately our decision (we Consumers) to render the final decision as to what we believe is safe to put into our body, or our children's. However, such an enormous responsibility can only be taken effectively, when our decisions regarding these Additives and Preservatives is based upon our having access to appropriate information relative to the same, including up-to-the-minute Research findings.

An example of the same might be Aluminum sulfate. Sold under the patent name of Alum. These colorless crystals are sweet to the taste, and have a drying effect in the mouth. Used for many years in detergents, Anti-Perspirants and as an antiseptic, in 1980 the Select Committee's report to the FDA stated that Aluminum sulfate should continue to remain on the GRAS (Generally Regarded As Safe) list. And it further stated that this additive should have "No Limitations" placed upon its use, other than those normal restrictions that were to be followed under "Good Manufacturing" practices.

These colorless, sweet-tasting little crystals however, are said to affect the human body's reproductive system, and are known to be mildly toxic either through injection or by ingestion.

PAFA~ *Priority Based Assessment of Food Additives. PAFA is the FDA'Ss Data Bank wherein toxicology information regarding chemicals is held.*

SELECT COMMITTEE~ This is a Committee selected by the FDA to review available information on various products and chemicals, and to report back to the FDA with their findings.

WHO~ The World Health Organization is an authorized Committee which is set up for the purpose of reviewing facts and information regarding specific products, and present their findings and opinions to the FDA upon completion of the same. They provide many books written by experts in the field, and cover such specific products as those that have recently been approved, banned, or pending approval. They would be happy to mail you a catalog upon request. In Washington D. C., they can be reached at (202)-974-3000.

COMMUNITY-RIGHT-TO-KNOW ~

The Government makes it mandatory that all Manufacturers who use toxic chemicals (such as Cyanide which is used in the manufacture of some food additives, including pesticides) must respond to the inquiries from employees, or citizens regarding the same. The U.S. Environmental Protection Agency, among other responsibilities, maintains a list of these compounds, and the Manufacturer's who use them.

EPA~ Environmental Protection Agency. This is an Agency which has several duties or responsibilities, and has delegated local Agencies for each geographic area. They help to preserve and maintain endangered species, protect wetlands preservation (including the natural inhabitants of these wetlands), and as mentioned above, they investigate toxic materials, or their use within their domain.

NTP~ National Toxicology Program

NRC~ National Research Council

National Academy Of Sciences~

The FDA became aware in the 1970's that well over one-hundred Laboratories that were providing Testing information to them, had a number of problems within their Laboratory Systems. In the 1980's, there were fraud charges filed against many of the executives who ran these Laboratories, stemming from contradictory, or inaccurate data that had been submitted to the FDA requesting approvals for Food Additives. But the submissions handed over by these executives from various Laboratories provided information which was erroneous, or inadequate, and prevented the FDA officials from reaching a valid decision regarding the Additives in question. In order to irradiate this type of unacceptable maneuvering from repeating itself, in 1980 the National Toxicology Program (NTP) contracted with two other Agencies; The National Academy of Sciences, and the (NRC) The National Research Council. Together, their goal was to accomplish two tasks; 1.- To establish the criteria for "Toxicity Testing" requirements involving substances that would inevitably be in ingested by humans, and 2.- To determine the level of toxicity of those substances being tested.

Another of their public safety goals was to develop and institute a uniform system whereby guidelines could be established according to priority of substance testing, and research into those substances which hold the greatest threat upon the public's health.

PAFA~ The FDA'S Data Bank. The FDA'S Bureau of Foods has created and organized a computerized Data Bank named PAFA, or Priority Based Assessment of Food Additives. The responsibility of this Data Bank is to collect, and store all of its toxicology information in an organized Bank, listing specific Classifications, and categories of food additives. Though it does not include Indirect food additives, or food contaminants, including those that are thought to be natural food constituents, the FDA would like to .include those categories in the future. Presently, there are nearly 3,000 additives on file in the data bank

WHO~ The World Health Organization is an Expert Committee on Food Additives. They meet with other Expert Organizations such as (FAO) The Food Agriculture Organization of the United Nations in order to share findings and set standards, amongst other agenda items.

These two Committee's are in agreement with the relationship of residues of specific additive substances found in drugs, animal medications, or in aids used to enhance animal production, as well as the frequency to which consumers are exposed, hence "*The Accumulative effect!*"

INDEX